MW01284932

REMOTE FEARS *& SILVER LININGS*
In all of life's challenge there comes a Silver Lining…
Can you find it?

Kimberly Arms Shirk
silverliningswriter@gmail.com
www.kimberlyshirk.com

DENVER, COLORADO

This book is dedicated to my family whose unconditional love carried me through. Chad, Mom & Dad, Randy & Angie, Valerie & Nathan, your encouragement never fails. Caleb, Logan & Addison you bring me constant joy.

Table of Contents

Acknowledgements

It's the Anniversary of my accident and after running off some unwanted memories, I've decided today is the day to write the forward to my book.

A good friend wished me "Happy Anniversary" today. We were standing in the middle of school and at first I had to pause. It wasn't June 28th, the day I married my best friend and husband, Chad. It wasn't even August, when he proposed. And then it dawned on me. It was September 3rd, many years after the accident that would define my life; my career, my faith, my every relationship with family and friends, my face and body, and most importantly my heart.

Tears leapt to my eyes, as they do about this time every year; mourning for what I have lost: a career I loved, my face, my leg, my sight, a naiveté about the world around us and the everyday dangers that lurk everywhere. Memories flooded of the countless days and weeks and months spent in the hospital and then recovering from five successive years of surgery. My heart sank thinking about what this day must mean to those closest to me…my mom, dad, brother and sister and husband, Chad. Or are they blessed to be oblivious to it all?

And yet my friend said, "Happy Anniversary!" She called it a miraculous celebration and recalled to me yet another detail I'd forgotten in the passage of time or the confusion of too many details. And so today, this book for me becomes a reality, not just in gathered thoughts sitting somewhere in the recesses of my mind and computer, but a mission I MUST finish. Quickly. Before the chalkboard of time erases all of the details I want to pass on to my three beautiful children. Before the urgency to educate and inspire others sinks into complacency of the every day.

There are far too many people to thank on this blank page. I truly will never get this book done if I try to remember everyone, so please know that I know who you are, and think of you often, perhaps more than you will ever know. But I am going to try my best to name some. To my many talented and gifted friends who have read a draft or another draft, or a chapter or another chapter in this storied journey and offered advice and encouragement. To my life-long, college friend, Cami, whose encouragement and daylong writing session inspired me to dust off my notes and get it done. To Cydney, Jim, and Kimberly at Talent Plus who took their precious time, and I do mean precious, to read, critique, discuss and offer encouragement along the way. To my dear friend Mandy, whose love of the written word and depth of knowledge about who I am deep down encouraged me to reveal my true self. To Dana, Michelle, and Julie, Apt. 37 crew. You inspire me every day with your intelligent conversation and encouragement. How blessed I am that our paths crossed so many years ago.

To my family and close friends, who entertained in their own way my requests to write, email, describe, or have a conversation with me about what they remember of the early days of my accident when my mind was not all there. To the many nurses, doctors, lab technicians, medical staff in general -- both the clinical who performed life-saving procedures and the non-clinical personnel who made sure I had clean sheets -- thank you for holding my health in such high esteem.

To Steven and JD and all of your friends, thank you for literally giving me the shirt off your back, I will never forget your sacrifice. To everyone mentioned in this book…you have played a significant role in my life and I'm forever in debt. To my cousin Stephanie, whose eye for graphic design and genuine love for me designed such a meaningful book cover. To my friend and colleague Aaron, who helped me with the formatting and all things technical that I don't do.

To Dr. Mark Reece and Sheila Borwick. There are no words. You saved me in every way you knew how and I am forever grateful. To Nathan and Angie, how incredibly grateful I am that you are my family and you stood beside me even before it was official. To my brother Randy, you inspire me each day with your love of God and the way you are able to communicate that with your words and actions. To my sister, Valerie, I cannot imagine life without you, you are a true sister in every meaningful way; encourager, listener, shoulder, and contagiously optimistic to your core. Mom, you are my pillar of strength, the one who still knows me best and can somehow inspire me even when we're miles apart. The gifts you and Dad have given each one of us are treasures more than diamonds and gold. I only wish I had finished this in time for Dad to read it himself. Dad, you never left my side and you carried me through. To Chad, my best friend, my rock, my fun. Your love of life, your constant presence have lifted me up far more than you will ever know.

To God, my Heavenly Father, I am rendered speechless when I think of your majesty, your all-knowing power, and the love you show me every day as one of your children.

Thank you all for helping me fight through my most Remote Fears and find my Silver Linings.

Today is the day that I have to tell my story…the one I've been preparing for so many years. Today is the day to tell my story. Is it yours?

> *"No temptation has seized you but what is common to man. And in this life we will be tempted. But God is faithful. When you are tempted He will give you a way out."*
>
> *1 Corinthians 10:13*

It became a favorite verse of mine in 1989, well I guess technically it was 1990. My friends had been killed on New Year's Eve night in a fire that ripped through the house, leaving no trace of life behind. A house I had been in just hours before. And in the early hours of the morning when I was getting calls about the accident, in a move of desperation, I reached for my Bible. *Give me an answer* was more an urgent plea than a prayer of any kind, and there beneath my blurred vision it was…a verse that would define my life.

He was true to His word that day. Those weeks, months, years that flew by and blurred once again my vision of the charred remains of my friends. Life dulled the pain of that day, and in that moment on New Year's Eve, God gave me a gift far beyond those words in scripture.

He implanted in me a belief that I could get through anything, not by just muddling through, but molded in just the way He wanted, just the way He planned. He gave me vision to see Silver Linings. They're everywhere. Can you see them?

Prologue: **HIGH VOLTAGE**

The thing about flames of fire is they engulf you. Good or bad, illuminating light or inflicting pain, wrapping you in warmth or strangling you with terror. It takes over and scars you undeniably for life. It's a ripple effect and often the remnants are your choice...ashes that blow away with a single breath or light dancing until the dawn, illuminating your very soul.

3000 volts of electricity can kill a man, sometimes less.

It should've been any other day at KLKN-TV8, where I had been a reporter and morning anchor for a year. We had our parking space marked off early. It helped that the television station was literally blocks from the State Penitentiary because the parking lot was exceptionally full tonight. There was little room to move between vehicles. Remote live trucks from across the state stood side by side a slew of spectators waiting to witness the events of the night.

What a relief it was to have our engineer on sight. As he drug out yards of cable, lifted the mast and squared away the camera equipment, I was freed up to do my job... to review my notes, practice my intro and seek out on-site interviews. My favorite parts of the job by far!

I never was very technically minded. I learned the bare minimum to accomplish what I needed. Beyond where does the microphone plug into the camera, I just wanted someone else to be in charge of making sure the reports I gave got back to the station and on air.

It was an unusual night. It's not often that you found a crowd at the State Pen. And usually when you did it meant big news. Tonight was no exception.

It was a warm evening in July of 1996, but there was a chill to the night. We had set up the remote live truck just before the 5 o'clock news amidst a swarm of other television stations all competing for the same view, the same story. The view wasn't spectacular at all. I found myself outside a gray non-descript building, fairly ordinary other than the spiked barbed wire that undeniably was meant to keep me out…or others in. What was spectacular in an eerie sort of way was the assembled crowd divided like the Red Sea and corralled on two separate sides.

"Die Joubert Die!" chanted one side. They were cheering for a man to die. I had been a part of many boisterous crowds fired up over one event or another; cheering on their team at a football game, or angered by the way their tax dollars were being spent. But other crowds were not quite like this one. Never before had I witnessed cheering that lead into a celebration of a man's death. "Justice Served" was the banner they held to my right, a raucous crowd relishing in what was to take place.

"Death Heals Nothing" was the cry of the opposing left side. The crowd was a mixture of people praying for God to intercede and this act to stop and furious voices, all directed across the parking lot.

There I stood in the crossfire, a dull sense of doing my job mingled with an overwhelming cloud hanging over me. "Hold on to perspective," I told myself as I walked the line between real life events and these surreal surroundings.

I was reporting that night from the Nebraska State Penitentiary and the only job more undesirable for me that night was to witness what was about to take place inside the walls of that building. The death penalty carried out.

I loved reporting the news. Giving people analysis of the very present happenings in our city at any given moment was rewarding and challenging. Especially exciting was the immediacy of going *live*. My script would be made of fiercely scribbled notes in a reporter's notebook. Several interviews with witnesses turned quickly into carefully crafted words all with the goal of bringing some clarity and objectivity to the audience sitting at home.

I loved the challenge and I was pretty good at it, but tonight was different. I wondered if I was becoming part of the story instead of merely reporting it. Did my presence at the scene, along with all of the other media stations, entice others to this anger on both sides? We were talking about a man's life.

I had done my homework.

"A large crowd has gathered here tonight to witness what they can see of the death penalty being resumed in Nebraska. It's been thirty-five years since the state has carried out a death sentence and as you can see behind me, it has drawn a crowd. Local authorities have gone to great lengths to keep the crowd separated tonight and hope to maintain order and peace outside the State Pen. There are literally barriers separating both advocates of the death penalty and those who oppose it. And you can hear their chants in the background. "We're told that in the next 30 minutes, child killer John Joubert will be executed." In 1984, Joubert was convicted of killing 13-year-old Danny Jo Eberle, and 12-year-old Christopher Walden.

Executions in Nebraska, after a 35-year hiatus, had resumed, leaving boisterous crowds wanting revenge and craving peace. And this story had quite a following. Court records from the trial indicated that Danny Jo Eberle was a paperboy whose papers never got delivered. And Christopher Walden's pleas for mercy fell on deaf ears as this murderous man stabbed him 9 times virtually decapitating him. So tonight for some was the chance to witness justice served, and for others raised questions of the virtue of the death penalty. But these ideologies had no bearing on my reporting. The fact was that tonight a man would meet his fate with the flip of a switch. And it was my job to report it.

It seemed surreal to me that the gathered crowd would return to their daily lives tomorrow. They would make their way to homes and jobs and the buzz of the night would dissolve into just another news cycle. But was there something more to this night? Something I could sense but not quite put my finger on. Why was this night so vivid in my mind?

I was there that night at the penitentiary and I reported the coverage the next day.

"Child killer John Joubert, died last night at 12:29 a.m. in Nebraska's State Penitentiary."

3000 volts of electricity can kill a man, sometimes less. The muscles contract, and grip paralysis. Respiratory systems shut down. First comes heart fibrillation and then it clamps tight. Tissue and organs burn and then death.

Less than 3000 volts killed a killer that night. 13,200 volts didn't kill me.

1
To Tell A Story

Journalism seemed a natural fit for my interests in writing, speaking, theater, film and photography. I had no interest in being an English major, where opportunities might seem endless but not very clear or practical. And I loved a good story. I could find one almost anywhere, and I loved organizing information to make it succinct. So journalism was my first and only major in college. I threw myself into daily performances on TV using my brain.

I graduated from the University of Nebraska-Lincoln with a Bachelor's degree in Broadcast Journalism, aptly renamed "Electronic Media" by the time graduation rolled around. I spent years writing and re-writing copy, editing to make it shorter, framing a picture in my mind and framing a picture through a camera lens. I loved the creativity it allowed me to tell a story dramatically, but also the practical ways of television. I knew each day a story had to be told in one minute and thirty seconds, or often less.

I began my career at Fox 42 in Omaha, NE, as an editor. I was good at my job, but never technologically savvy. I preferred being on the street and talking to people, so when a job as a reporter came open,

I jumped at it. I was the true one-man band: carrying equipment, shooting the story, shooting my own stand-up, writing the story, editing the story and often running camera for the newscast afterward.

It was grueling work, but I loved watching the finished product and pitching new story ideas for upcoming days. I especially loved comparing my stories to those produced by other, more experienced reporters at bigger stations. Often, we had covered the same angle and sometimes I found an interview or shot they didn't get. I loved the challenge of competing nose-to-nose with other stations and winning.

When a new television station was starting up in Lincoln, Nebraska, I leapt at the chance to do reporting and anchoring back in my college town. Literally building KLKN-TV8 from the ground up was exciting and rewarding. While we skirted construction of the building and set, we would introduce the news staff to the Governor or various businesses and non-profits. We had a role with the news director in choosing the graphics and musical intros for the newscasts and we were trained on the brand new equipment. The beginnings were thrilling and high energy. Everyone was on board to make it a success and everyone was watching to see if we would.

After a few months, the newness began wearing off. While I worked mostly with colleagues I respected and thought highly of, I also found myself in the throes of what I didn't like about a newsroom.

A newsroom can be an eclectic mix of egos, vanity, intelligence of varying levels and big talkers. Everyone is competing for face time, and unfortunately, it's not always about the story you have to tell, but the face time you get before the camera. While I competed for the lead story, I was constantly bothered by the lack of commitment to what I deemed "real" news stories. I would often pitch complex stories only to be shot down because it would "take too much time" to research that story, or it was sweeps month and my story idea wasn't sexy enough.

The most egregious example came when I was told that a story about a local company trying to overcharge their customers had to be toned down because they were valuable advertisers. I had no patience for this. Were we or were we not in the business of reporting the truth?

I remember a conversation with a newspaper reporter colleague of mine where I lamented the fact that he had an entire afternoon to sift through legislative bills to seek out a story. In contrast, I had to grab a sound bite, a shot of the chamber and lug my heavy equipment back to the station to write a VOSOT (voice over sound on tape) for the midday cast. Then somehow I needed to draw an entire story out of that single sound bite for the five, six and ten o'clock news, while simultaneously writing three other stories.

As disappointing as that was, it didn't even touch the vanity issue. I was fortunate enough to work with some real pros in those first two stations who cared more about the story than their make-up. I also came across some others, who couldn't craft a story if it hit them in the face. Incredibly, those same people often saw more face time than I ever imagined.

I was dismayed by this thought before I ever went into journalism. Men could somehow age 40 years, gain a significant amount of weight and still anchor the nightly news, yet when a woman crossed the threshold of about 30, she was quickly demoted to the morning shift or "Special Assignments."

There was so much hypocrisy in the everyday at the newsroom.

People who were diligent and effective were taken advantage of so that others could look good. Good stories were buried for the latest eye catching crime statistic. News directors were run down by the latest order that required them to go above and beyond what the newsroom was staffed to accomplish. Consistently they were asked to staff and provide equipment for a news staff with little funding. The expectation to cover the news in a 24 hour news cycle with bare bones staffing, rundown equipment and nearly no budget was almost laughable or a crime. Generally, they were good people who loved the news and were misplaced in a management role.

The flip side of the obstacles in the newsroom, were the remarkably motivating moments. I was inspired by the stories of people I could tell each day. At my first television station out of college, I created a weekly series to highlight stellar students who had talent beyond their years. We weren't just looking for the standout student in academia, sports or music, but really in leadership. For me, sharing their stories weekly was what was right about the news.

I was also fortunate enough to have worked side-by-side with some incredibly intelligent people. Authentic, genuine and straightforward reporters and anchors who were passionate about getting it right... every time. Their dedication to the craft of journalism, verifying and protecting sources, providing an unbiased and objective version of the stories of the day, was inspiring. For those journalists, who relished the story and sought every day to tell the truth, now that was a group I wanted to be a part of. For me, the good outweighed the bad, so though there was plenty to be distraught about, I had been bitten by the bug. And as any good journalist will tell you, once you have it in your blood, it's remarkably hard to give it up.

Despite what I had seen in some newsrooms or heard about from friends working in other markets, I was fortunate enough to work with some real pros. Dedicated journalists committed to reporting the truth, whether or not it happened to be their opinion. They were married to the facts and presenting thought-provoking stories. I learned from some great mentors, the value of keeping your word and the real importance of being confidential to a source who had the courage to report a story that might not be favorable to their own organization. I also knew the power of the written word. Power that could be used for great good and power that could be used to tear down and never repair. It was a power that I took seriously with every word that I wrote and the challenge of presenting the many sides of a story and thinking big picture about some serious topics intrigued me from the beginning.

So when I sat in the office of my soon-to-be new boss at WOI-TV5 and listened to him describe the job, although my radar went up, it didn't ring loudly enough to prevent me from taking that fateful step.

WOI-TV5

I was married in June of 1997, to my best friend in college, Chad. We moved to Des Moines right after our honeymoon. Chad was a banker, a numbers guy, the antithesis of his creative, artsy but practical wife, and we were a perfect fit. He was the eternal optimist, laid back, fun, outdoorsy husband, while I was the practical, thoughtful, reserved and analytical wife. We had a great time together. He made me fun and I made him think. Chad was in a management-training program with Norwest Bank at the time and so we moved to Des Moines, Iowa, and I went looking for a job.

Fortunately, my former station had a sister station, owned by the same company, in Des Moines. They had an opening, so I was going to interview for that job. Other stations in Des Moines caught my attention immediately for being more professional and more widely watched, but we knew we would only be there a short time and WOI seemed a decent fit. Plus, I loved the news director.

This was a man who knew news and cared about it. I remember the interview clearly. We had an intelligent conversation about the value of news and where we projected its future. We talked politics, world news and economics. I immediately decided that he was one of the good ones. So although I expressed concern about the part of the job description that stated I would assist in running a live truck from time to time, I trusted this man. I believed that he would not put me in that position before I felt comfortable.

Two weeks after I was hired, he quit.

Chad and I worked opposite schedules. He worked the 8-5, or so he said. I maintain it was really 8:00 - 3:30 and then social time after that. I worked the night shift, which in the newsroom was about 3-11. I would go into the station in the afternoon and get an assignment. Some days it was reporting, some days it was shooting for someone else. And that was okay for now. I had only been at the station a few months and felt like my work had proven itself. I'd even approached the General Manager about doing some anchor run-throughs hoping to fill in for vacationing anchors.

I gained the respect of our chief photographer by proving I could shoot and edit even his stuff. Even our seasoned reporter-turned-news director complimented some of my work. I was beginning to feel that this would be a place to get some good Live experience. I had done some live shots in Lincoln, but not nearly as often as I wanted. There is no better practice for live shots other than to do them over and over. This was exactly what I needed to bolster my audition tape and to jump to a new level at my next job. Though it wasn't my first love, I tolerated shooting for other reporters and even volunteered every once in a while to help out. So in the beginning of September when I was assigned to be a photographer, I didn't think much of it.

My colleague, David Bingham, was working on a story about church vandalism for the five o'clock news. He was scheduled for a live shot from the church at the top of the hour. I returned to the station and the photographer that was assigned to shoot David's live shot was called away to a fire. As he raced past me in the newsroom I remember the conversation.

"What's wrong David?" I asked.

"I don't know how I'm gonna get it all done," he said as he flew past me to grab some extra notes from his desk. *"My photographer just got called away to a fire and I need to get there now."*

"What do you still need to do? Where's your live shot?" I asked.

"I can help." I looked at a colleague to make sure she was ok with that, since I had been assigned to help her tonight.

"Just grab equipment and get there. Des Moines Christian School." he responded.

That split second decision to help a colleague would change my entire life.

The newsroom is where my memory of that day and the weeks to come ends.

2
Four Minutes

On this particular day it was beautiful outside. The sun was shining brightly and preparing to begin it's decent and duck behind the horizon. The time of day was near 4:45 p.m. I began setting up the equipment; tripod, microphones, camera balanced and ready to shoot.

Then, the mistake happened, and my memory goes blank. I don't remember riding to the church in the Live van. Not setting the camera or microphones up. Not the explosion that followed when David was initially struck by the electricity.

David began to raise the forty-foot mast on our live truck. *Whaam!*

" '…I was watching them put up their mast,' (said Gary Mattix, an eyewitness to the event), 'I got within 10 yards of the van and I heard an explosion. I saw (Bingham) go under the van and he burst into flames. I stopped the truck and jumped out and (Arms) came around the van and saw her buddy.' He speculated that Arms might have been shocked when she leaned against the van as she tried to save Bingham." (Des Moines Register, September 4, 1997.)

After the huge explosion, the second fate-tempting mistake took place.

I would later learn that all safety standards would indicate that I did exactly the opposite of what I should have done. I should have stayed away. I should have called for help. And if I had followed those safety standards, likely David would now be dead. I can only assume my heart won out.

I ran from the opposite side of the van to find out what happened. Though it's unclear whether I reached out to help David or whether the electricity drew me into him, one thing is clear: The force of the 13,200-volt electrical line had found a grounding path -- first through David and then coursing through me. Electrical force drew both of us underneath the van. My head hit the electrified van and I burst into flames. The sheer force of the electricity was too much for our bodies to contain.

The accident occurred outside of a church that doubled as a Christian School, and students were waiting for their rides home. Immediately, several students ran to our aid, while others called 911. Though some adult witnesses were screaming for the teenagers to stay away, these Christian students miraculously pulled us away from the van. In that brave moment, they brought us one step closer to safety.

Because electricity travels in concentric circles, if you connect with the circles of electrical current and are not insolated with a non-conductive surface, you will become a transmitter of the electrical charge and possibly drawn into the originating source of electricity. The human body is a major conductor of electricity, so as the students came to my rescue, their protection can only be described as protection of some sort. I choose to believe it was a miracle.

Stephen Myers was 16 years old at the time. He had taken charge that day. He shouted for his brother to call 911 while he threw off his shirt to put out the flames consuming my body. He and his 14-year-old brother, JD, would be interviewed at the scene minutes after they had taken David and me to the hospital. Visibly shaken, the two recounted what they experienced.

> *"They were both on fire. I tried to put out the flames and then turned them on their sides to keep them from choking. He was conscious and breathing. She, well I don't think she was conscious, she was just breathing. They're bad off. She was burnt where the fire had gotten to her, but not moving, not conscious at all…just breathing,"* were the choked up words of Myers, spoken as he tried to process what had just happened.

In the time it took the first paramedics to arrive, some decided I was dead. The first EMTs on the scene took one look at me and moved on, concluding the same thing. My injuries were so severe, that in the split-second mandatory analysis that occurs every day in the life of paramedics, the decision was made to let me die and fight for my colleague.

I didn't like that decision. I wasn't ready to go. So I fought. And fortunately, four minutes later a second set of EMTs arrived on the scene and gave me a chance.

David was conscious and irritated. His medics were trying to get basic information from him, asking him if he knew his wife's name. As he struggled physically with what was happening, he would shout, *"Kim, her name is Kim."*

The medics knew that was my name and responded to David, *"No, that's your colleague's name,"* thinking I was likely already dead and wanting to draw attention away from what was happening.

David, as sharp as ever, was able to adamantly respond, *"No, I KNOW that, but my wife's name is also Kim!"* He was right. David was loaded into the ambulance and rushed to a nearby hospital.

My injuries were grave. When my head hit the van I burst into flames and it took the brave actions of those high school students to put them out. Fortunately, the second set of EMTs set to work. They raised my limp body onto a stretcher and immediately listened for a heartbeat. A "clean sinus rhythm" would bring great comfort to my mom, a registered nurse, when she first learned of my injuries.

I was not conscious, my heart beating, yes and breathing, but not able to respond at all. After they loaded the dead weight of my burnt body into the ambulance, they raced for help and a sign of hope. I was taken to Iowa Methodist Medical Center, a different location from David, with a more sophisticated burn center.

Later, the doctors would confirm the severity of my injuries. My burns were the most severe in degree and covered twelve to fifteen percent of my body. While the percentage in itself was not life threatening, the path the electricity chose was.

I suffered third and fourth degree burns to my entire left leg from the top of my thigh to the end of my toes. Both feet suffered burns. My doctors would identify these as exit points for the electricity after it had traveled through my body and down my leg.

My left knee also suffered severe damage. The electricity, in its path racing through my body, decided my knee was a hindrance and nearly disintegrated the cartilage and muscle behind my kneecap.

Those burns, although significant, were not the greatest concern. My head came into contact with the electrified van and the right side of my head was burned down to the skull from the impact. The days immediately following my accident were crucial as doctors monitored me closely while my brain swelled.

The path the electricity took was obvious to doctors as they saw in a picture they took that first day. Concentric circles fanned out from the initial impact point that burned to my skull. A small part of my ear was also burned beyond repair.

The extent of my injuries meant that I was a mess and would require untold hours in the operating room with no evident positive result. But as God directs patients to fight, I believe he inspires doctors and nurses to fight just as hard, even when the light of hope seems incredibly dim. And so I began the journey of spending hours in the operating room immediately with a team of dedicated and talented clinical surgeons.

The days that followed September 3rd were treacherous by all accounts. Physicians, unsure of my prognosis, did what they could to minimize my injuries and provide an opportunity to heal, unsure of the end game.

My left great toe was partially amputated, but doctors were able to save my other limbs and appendages. Although my kneecap remained in place, doctors had to reconstruct my knee using a third of my calf muscle from that same leg. To this day I cannot sustain any significant weight on that knee.

Neurosurgeons performed a craniotomy to relieve swelling and remove a dangerous blood clot. Following the removal of the blood clot from my brain, my neurosurgeon removed a portion of my skull, allowing my swelling brain to grow and eventually retract. My neurosurgeons then began the delicate process of removing a muscle from my back to cover the entire right side of my head. They then reconnected the blood supply to sustain my newly placed muscle. This would eventually allow me to grow hair on the right side of my head.

The severity of my injuries demanded that I would be placed in a medically induced coma for a month. Unbeknownst to me, my family stood vigil at my side. Waiting, waiting and more waiting for just a sign that I would wake up.

3
Out Of The Fog

Those days and weeks were long and hard for my family. Weeks went by filled with phone calls and well-intentioned visitors checking in, dropping by food and gifts. They wanted to bring comfort to my family and for that I am forever grateful. I believe they also wanted to embrace the reality of answered prayer, but day after day, that was not to be. Everyone wanted updates on my condition. I cringe at the thought of my family having to say "no change" day after day. The words must have caught in their throats as they tried to be gracious while they struggled through their own personal grief at the situation. But still they still hung on to a glimmer of hope that I would pull through this devastating accident. While visitors flooded the hospital seeking good news of my condition, my family stood in some combination of shock, disbelief and hope, hanging delicately in the balance of stunned, prayerful worry.

They met with doctors and heard cautionary tales of having too much hope that I would 1. Live and/or 2. Recover any semblance of my "normal" self.

When my immediate surgeries to my head, knee and feet had begun to heal, it was time to address the 12% of my body that sustained severe 3rd and 4th degree burns. That meant the tub room. Slowly, the nurses weaned me off of some of the paralytic drugs.

The day I thought I woke up, was not really the day I woke up. My husband and parents, who had literally moved into the waiting room just outside of the burn unit, remember things differently. Based on the sheer number of narcotics in my system at the time, I'm going to trust their memories over mine.

This was the day I woke up. But this day, my first day, I remember nothing, but my Dad did…

> "The most amazing thing I've ever experienced spiritually happened the night of 9/28. Usually my prayers are private and relatively short. Always were. The night before you woke up, I lay down in bed in Omaha and prayed for what must have been 20 minutes or more, the most intensely personal prayer to Jesus I've ever prayed, that He would bring you back to us I don't even recall if I asked Him to bring you back in an "normal" state, just to bring you back so that we could tell you how much we loved you and missed you in our midst.
>
> The next day I had a voice mail from Mom, 'Kim woke up to-day!!!! She sat on the side of the bed with virtually little help from the nurses, stood up and took six steps to a chair. Your eyes were wide open. An occupational therapist came in for ten minutes of questions. Knew her name, birthday, roughly the time of year it was and the names of her brother and sister. Responded to virtually every question asked, used her hands for sign language that she learned in college though no one understands it yet! After her bath wheeled in a sitting position

in a chair to door where Judy (mom) and Randy (brother) were, them not knowing all this was happening. You waved to them!

You couldn't talk yet, but were mouthing words. You were getting tired. You wanted to see Chad (imagine!) and he got there immediately from his office. You stayed awake almost all day.

The doctors and we were all elated to see your physical and mental responses. Had all the nurses in tears.' I drove to Des Moines that evening."

Then they transported me into the tub room, to clean my burns.

Burn victims and those that know of them, know this to be an excruciatingly painful time. In a process that can take hours, they carefully remove bandages, wash and remove every bit of dead skin in order to allow new skin to form. Then nurses reapply all the protective medicines and bandages, until the next day. I would soon know it as an exhausting pattern of daily routine. My bath literally took over an hour as they moved from the top of my head to the tips of what was left of my toes.

A SPIRITUAL WALK

Chad and I were still new to town and had not yet joined a church. We visited several, often knowing right away that it wasn't a good fit for us. Maybe the message was not quite on, or the congregation seemed more stalker-like than just friendly, too small, too big. We had only been there for about four weeks and having come from a church home we loved, I wasn't willing to jump into membership too quickly. We did however visit a church that felt very much like home. A friend from work had suggested it, it was where she and her husband attended, and so we went to one service. It was a beautiful Presbyterian church with an amazing choir and phenomenal stained glass windows. I don't honestly remember the message from the day, but I do have a picture of walking out that day being greeted by a young and very tall Pastor, who welcomed us and invited us to come back. I didn't have the chance to grace the halls of that church again…instead they came to me.

An angel, who doubled as the Pastor from Iowa Presbyterian Church, happened to be visiting that day. That's not true. Actually, he had visited since the first day I was brought in.

GOLF

The night of my accident Chad was called off of the golf course. He will forever proclaim, "It was the best golf game of my life," although if I could give you a nickel for every time I've heard that in the years since I've known Chad, I'd be richer than Warren Buffet.

Chad and several of his work buddies, as they often did, headed out for a round of golf after their training program was finished for the day. Another colleague, Brooke happened to be at home watching the news on Channel 5. She wasn't a golfer.

> "We at WOI-TV5 are saddened to report to you that two of our colleagues were preparing to report a story for our five o'clock news when the mast of the Remote Live Truck came into contact with electrical lines. We are attempting to be in contact with their families and will report to you on their conditions as soon as possible."

Brooke knew immediately that was the station I worked for, as she often saw more of my stories than Chad did. When the anchor returned to report our names, she knew exactly where he was. She called the golf course and asked for Chad. She knew him well enough to say, *"He'll tell you he'll call me later, but tell him it's an emergency!"* True to form, when the cart girl at the golf course rolled up to say he had an important call from Brooke, he said, *"Please tell her I'll call her back."* She insisted it was an emergency and Chad got on the phone to hear from Brooke, *"I think Kim's been in an accident. She's been taken to Iowa Methodist Medical Center. Get there fast!"*

Never again will I get my husband off of the golf course that quickly.

IOWA METHODIST MEDICAL CENTER

Having just lived there for a short time, Chad didn't even really know where Iowa Methodist was, but he managed to find it and walk into a hospital lobby full of media. All four stations were covering the story of church vandalism that night so the three major networks, ABC, NBC, CBS and FOX all had reporters on the scene, if not when the accident happened, shortly afterwards. Reporters from the Des Moines Register were also on hand, each one trying to hear the latest on our conditions. Chad knew two people in the room. Brooke, who had gone there immediately after she got ahold of Chad and our dear friend Brian. Brian was a friend from college, a roommate of Chad's before we got married, and an usher in our wedding. He met him at the door and told him, *"I think you need to talk to a chaplain."* It was hospital policy for any family member hearing news of another family member for the first time to talk to a chaplain first. Chad happened to get a chaplain on his very first day of the job, ever.

"What's going on with my wife?" Chad urgently asked.

"It's too crowded in here, let's go somewhere a little more private," he said.

Chad followed him to a busy waiting room.

"It's too busy here." And they moved on to another room.

When it looked like he was going to move again, Chad grabbed his arm and interrupted.

"I don't care if we go to the ladies bathroom, you need to tell me what happened to my wife!"

The chaplain was so shaken, he simply handed Chad my burnt clothes, my burnt shoes and the cross necklace I was wearing.

"Is she dead?" Chad muttered.

"No, no, she's in the burn unit, but it's very serious, "he managed to get out.

"Take me to her!" Chad demanded.

Then the new chaplain proceeded to get Chad lost in the hallways of the large hospital.

SECOND BAPTISM

Enter, the angel Pastor from the Iowa Presbyterian church. My colleague from work had called her pastor to tell him what happened and he dropped everything and came straight to the hospital. There he found Chad wandering with the aimless Chaplain and took him right where he needed to go.

This man, who didn't even know us, found Chad the night of my accident and guided him to my bedside. This man was an angel to me, though I didn't know it at the time. He had helped my new husband through what was the start of an extremely difficult, long and slow race.

And so the Pastor was back again this day, as he had been, visiting with my family. He was one of the many visitors who would grace the waiting room in those difficult days. Some would file in, speak polite words of greeting, wait for my family to share some news, of which they had none, and then politely excuse themselves after a fair amount of uncomfortable silence. But this Pastor had taken my family under his wing. He had prayed with them, brought food and gifts from the congregation, spent time getting to know my family. And this day, he was there to celebrate. I had opened my eyes, squeezed some hands and I was alert enough for them to take me into the burn unit tub room.

This Pastor, a tall, gentle giant, had been praying for me since the day of my accident and had led an entire congregation in prayers for me. He was almost as thrilled to hear the news and celebrate with my family as they were.

"She's awake and they have taken her to the tub room," my mom explained with tears in her eyes."

"That's great news," he responded. "Mark today not just as the day she woke up, but also as her second baptism."

JUST BREATHE

I was baptized when I was 6 months old. Born with pneumonia, I was whisked away from my parents early on and kept at the hospital until I could sufficiently eat and breathe on my own. This was an especially difficult time for my mom, as any mother can imagine. You wait a very long 9-10 months to deliver your child and when she's born she is taken from you. But she remained strong and eventually I was returned to her loving arms.

Now twenty-six years later, my mom stood vigil for an even longer period of time. It was over a month of waiting this time to see if I would return. And if I did, who would I be? Would I remember her caring arms, her words of wisdom, her name or face? Today was a victory to be sure: my second baptism. She knew the journey ahead would be long, bumpy and fraught with pain and scarring.

As a registered nurse, my mom was equipped with knowledge beyond those of us who take our health for granted. When doctors or nurses would flex some medical pretense surrounding my case, she relied on her nursing instinct to make decisions on my behalf. Resourceful, kind and incredibly intelligent, although she had retired from nursing, she counted us -- me, my brother and sister -- as her prize patients. In her humility, whether she would acknowledge it or not, her extensive knowledge bank and experience would be in full use for years to come.

For today, that journey was stored in the back of her mind. For now, it was enough to celebrate a bath.

THE JOB AHEAD

From the moment she arrived at the hospital, my mom was laser focused on my recovery. I'm not sure there was a moment she didn't think I'd pull through. My parents were traveling home from a visit with my relatives in Texas as the immediate aftermath of my accident was unfolding. My sister and brother, having been notified by a friend, were trying frantically to get ahold of them, but in the very early days of cell phones, a drive from Texas to Nebraska could be remarkably quiet. Much later my mom would tell me that her years of Bible study had taught her to make the most of the silence. As she drove back, she spent time praying for each of her children. Minutes before my accident in Des Moines, my mom was praying for me, and safety at my job. As far as she knew, being a reporter in a strange city would take me to unknown neighborhoods as I covered a police beat or a crime scene. It could put me in close proximity to dangerous situations. She had no idea that God in His perfect timing would be hearing her prayers just as I needed them the most.

My mom was a nurse before she dedicated her life to raising her three children. She cared for our bumps and bruises, and our broken hearts. She cheered our victories and cried with us over defeats. You'd always find her volunteering at school, sitting in the bleachers at our games and driving us to piano lessons. She instilled in us a love of others and daily showed us that people mattered more than anything else in the world. She didn't just teach us that, she lived it. My sister recalls vividly a time at one of our games where a man, obviously drunk and possibly homeless sat at one of our games. He was babbling incoherently and while the other mothers ushered their children away, our mom walked right over to him and asked if she could help him. My mom was the Good Samaritan and her role as the caregiver and nurse in our lives was about to take hold once again.

My mom was not a gardener in the traditional sense of the word. In fact, I always felt like I inherited her genes when it came to inadvertently killing anything green. I would inevitably forget to water my plants for weeks on end and then when they looked so pathetic that I felt like I might have to throw them away, I would try in vain to recover them by overwatering them and nearly drowning the poor things.

I was never good at portion control. It was all or nothing for me when it came to plants or almost anything else in my life. That philosophy never seemed to work out in favor of the plants. I may have learned that lesson from my mom, but the other lessons she taught me far outweighed the less than stellar gardening skills.

My mom was a gardener of far more important things in my estimation. She was a gardener and caretaker to people's hearts and we happened to be the blessed benefactors. She would plant a seed, a thought in your mind and encourage you along the way until you thought it was your own. She would water that seed like a gentle rain, the kind you like to dance in and she would warm it like a ray of sunshine breaking through the clouds. When we started to outgrew ourselves, or showed a selfish side, and began thinking more of ourselves than others, she would prune us until we again found our thoughtful heads and hearts. She would celebrate with us when, with great strength we lifted one another up. My mom was, and continues to be, the ultimate encourager, listener, and she knew us better than we knew ourselves. In terms of growing people, she was unmatched in skill and talent and as intelligent and gifted a caretaker as anyone could imagine. Keeping a plant alive may never be her gift, but she was about to lead our family in keeping me alive.

OF COURSE I KNOW YOU

The first day I remember being "awake" I was wheeled out into the waiting room. My family had called this sterile, slightly cramped, room home for over a month. It happened that some neighbors of my parents from Omaha had come to visit that day. It was a party of sorts. Strangest party I've ever attended. Draped in a yellow hospital gown, I was wheeled out in a wheelchair. My weight, I later learned, had dropped below 100 pounds and all my muscle was gone, atrophied from being in a coma for over a month. My head was fully covered with white bandages. Underneath I no longer had hair, half of it burned off in the injury, never to naturally return, and the other half shaved off before surgery. I've never had color to my skin. My sister, Valerie, who has beautiful complexion and always tans easily, affectionately called me Casper, and she was right. But now, after lying still in a hospital bed and already undergoing several life-saving surgeries. Any color I did have was literally drained out of me. I'm quite sure I was a bandaged skeleton and quite frightening to see.

Several neighbors were sitting there when I came out. How sad it was the way they looked at me. After a few moments of silence, they came individually up to me. In halted language as if I didn't understand English and with extra volume in their voices, they broke their silence of shock. It was understandable as they looked at this virtual stranger who looked nothing like the young bride they had seen walk down the aisle just months before.

> *"Hi Kim, I'm Thama Knudsen, and I live down the street and across from you parents in Omaha." "Kim, I'm Linda King, and I live around the corner from your parents." And finally, "Kim, I'm Pat Wise and I live across the street from your parents."*

We moved around a lot growing up. Wherever the Union Pacific saw fit for my Dad to work, we went. My parents would call a "family meeting" and we knew that meant: it was time to move. That happened about every two years for a while. We claimed St. Louis as home because we had lived there a full five years, but that was an anomaly and eventually we landed relatively permanently in Nebraska. We had been in Omaha for nearly ten years, a long time in my estimation. I had finished high school, gone fifty miles down the road to college and all the while my parents lived in the same house on Barbara Circle.

So here we were, sitting in the visitors lounge with these women whose children I had grown up with. And yet, they were introducing themselves to me as if I had no idea who they were. I couldn't talk because of the tracheotomy and I had very little energy to do anything but blink and smile. What I clearly remember thinking was, "*Duh, my parents have lived there for ten years. I KNOW who you are! Are you all okay?*"

In fact, just the opposite was true. Although I could completely comprehend everything they said, they had no idea if I would. At that time, there was no promise that I would ever walk, talk, stand or even remember who my own family was, let alone the neighbors who had lived across the street from my parents for the past decade. Although my brain and heart wanted desperately to communicate, my body would not allow it. It's a strange thing to be trapped in yourself with no way to express thoughts. Today I was just an observer, unable to tell them they were wrong, I was still here…they just didn't know it yet.

The days ahead would prove frustrating, but for now, it was good enough to be out of the hospital bed.

It was a breakthrough day for me, that first day I remembered anything. Looking back, it was a breakthrough day for us all: Though I could not yet speak it, I was fully conscious and aware of everything going on around me.

For my family that knowledge came in exciting bits and pieces but slowly. After we began the rigorous therapy I would come to know as the norm, a therapist once asked if I wore glasses. "Of course I did," I wanted to shout, but stringing two words together was still a struggle. No one had thought about bringing my glasses to the hospital over the course of the last month. My mother asked Chad if he knew where my glasses were. I interrupted and wrote, "the second drawer down in the bathroom." Chad and I had lived in our one bedroom apartment for only two months, and yet I was able to recall the exact location of my glasses. My short-term memory was intact. What seemed to me another every-day detail, I certainly should have known was a great victory to my family. These were the early days when baby steps were giant leaps.

DR. REECE & HIS AVERTED EYES

My doctor wasn't convinced I would survive until that day. He averted his eyes when he spoke of my condition to my family. I remember the conversation with my mother well.

> "Your main doctor is Dr. Mark Reece. He was here the night you were brought in. He's a good doctor, but I'm not sure you're going to like him," my mother said when I was cohesive enough to understand. "I know how you like it when people look you in the eye when they speak to you, and, well, Dr. Reece doesn't do that."

It was a pet peeve of mine. I didn't like people who appeared to be having a conversation with you, while simultaneously looking past you. It was as if a more interesting conversation might be lurking around the next corner. I was convinced you could always tell when a politician was lying to you, because they would not hold your gaze when answering a tough question. So here I was prepared to meet my lead doctor. The man whose care I had been in and would continue to be in for years to come. In the two minutes I had to reflect on this conversation, inside, I already decided he was either extremely shy or incompetent. I wasn't thrilled about either option. Then I met Dr. Reece and I could not have been more wrong. My anxiety was completely unfounded!

According to my sister, *"The day you woke up, he found his smile."*

Dr. Mark Reece could not have been more competent, down to earth, forthright, knowledgeable, and slightly introverted, all with a great sense of humor! The fact was, unbeknownst to me at the time, my condition was so severe that his diagnosis was tentative. I defied my injuries at every turn. When electricity hit my head, I survived. When life-saving surgeries to decrease brain swelling were performed, I survived. When infection threatened my burns and my life once again, I survived. But when Dr. Mark Reece met my family, although I was in a medically-induced coma, in his mind, I had not yet survived. And so until he met me himself, his eyes were averted. Then I woke up. And he smiled.

CHILDREN

My family had to go through a routine cleansing every time they entered my room. Yellow hospital gowns ensured that infection would not enter my room. Face masks protected me from unintentional germs breathed on me. It was an antiseptic, sterilized and yet the room was aglow with the latest Crayola shades of red, green, blue and yellow. And those were just the pictures I saw. I awoke on September 29th to a room filled with well wishes from children. Cards hung throughout my hospital room, making it look more like an elementary school than a sterile hospital room.

The messages brought tears to my eyes as I read of a fourth grader telling me God would make me better and a fifth grader who was praying for me every night at the dinner table with his family. It was those messages that lined my walls and lit up my world in those first painful days. The cards that hit me most were those from the Des Moines Christian School, where the accident had taken place. Those fourth and fifth graders adopted me in a sense and took time out of their reading and writing to pray for me and send well wishes my way.

BABY STEPS

I've never liked reviews. The days before a big test from middle school to college always seemed to encompass a review. Basically going over once again what you were already expected to know. There was value in this, refreshing your memory for an upcoming test, but in my mind there was also excess. Wasted time when we could be learning something new was spent on the past...and if you did your work, which I always did, it was boring.

Imagine my surprise when I realized that the most trivial, rote, no-brainer activities were now going to be my course of study for the next 6 months. I was unable to talk at first, though I desperately wanted to communicate. My mother would spend hours with me trying to explain to an uncomprehending mind what had happened to me.

> "Honey, you've been in an accident, but we're with you now and everything's going to be alright. You're in a hospital in Des Moines and the doctors are taking good care of you."

There was a lot of emphatic pointing from me, a journalist whose questions had been stifled, and rudimentary charades played with multiple members of my family as they tried to understand what I was attempting to say.

When I was awake long enough to process minimal bits of information, I would start making sounds and gesturing wildly. For a reporter who constantly asked questions, there is little worse than the idea that you can't verbally communicate. My husband recognized this and brought me a white board to write on. I took the marker and wrote up and down that first day. My writing was illegible markings, no longer written horizontally, but instead vertically, convincing Chad that although pre-accident I could speak and write English rather well, I had woken up without words. He suspected I was writing an ancient language vertically, which no one could comprehend.

It's not hard to understand why my family couldn't answer my every question. My thoughts raced faster than I could communicate them. Not only could I not convey my questions clearly, but the exhaustion was endless. I could be mid thought and immediately fall asleep. In my fragile state, my brain was still not functioning clearly. Nights were the worst. That's when the dreams came.

They were frightening and felt real. These were intensely personal battles I shared with no one, unable to even process them myself. Although I couldn't have shared them if I tried because I still could not speak, I would react physically to them, thrashing in my sleep. Obviously they signaled outward signs of trouble to my family.

The most vivid horrifying dream I remember was so strange I didn't speak of it for years. To this day I cannot see any kind of scary movie or be near a haunted house. I can't even handle my children playfully chasing me up the stairs at night. It is frighteningly real to me and takes me back to a string of dark nights when I felt like I was trapped and couldn't get away.

4

The Gift of a Balloon

I tried to rationalize these dreams. I now know that medication plays a part. A constant stream of doctors and nurses would poke me with needles, thrust breathing treatments on me causing me to feel like I was suffocating, all the while an endless stream of helium-filled balloons danced in my room. At night, they were moving shadows, people who wanted to hurt me.

No flowers were allowed in my room. The risk of infection was simply too high. For burn patients, infection is a huge cause of death. So while the waiting room filled with food and flowers for my family to enjoy, the only thing allowed into my room were the cards and balloons. Friends filled with compassion wanted to do something, anything to help from afar, so they quickly filled my room, eventually enveloping the cards that hung on the wall, full of good intention and unintended fear. They were given of great concern and were so thoughtful and appreciated at that time especially by my family, but to me they were scary. Not only did the balloons that filled my room make it hard for the doctors to work but at night, combined with my heavy medications, they became frightening, dancing demons.

Once my family realized how frightening these were to me, Chad and my sister, Valerie, spent an entire day delivering balloons to patients on the children's hospital floors. For them, the result was positive. My screams subsided and I had peace when the balloons had a new home and were gone from my room. Just as I hoped, the frightening balloons disappearing from my room brought a decidedly different reaction on the opposite side of the hospital floor.

We shared a floor with children from the cancer ward and I knew that in the light of day, these helium-filled messages of joy had brought many smiles...and they would do the same for other children. So Chad and Valerie, my sister, had a job to do. They were to deliver the balloons to other children on the floor as a gift from me. At the time I could not move from my bed and my husband and sister graciously became my hands and feet.

Chad would tell me of the trips they made. Smiles were put on faces of children whose days were filled with only doctors and medical tests. Even young children who didn't seem to understand what was going on would smile at the delivery of a balloon. But there was one little boy who wanted to do something more...he wanted to give something back.

I remember the conversation so clearly. The curtains were drawn and the door closed as the nurses were extremely cautious about who could enter my room, but this day there was a knock. My mother went to the door and found a small young boy. He asked if he could meet me, he had a present to give to me. When my mom told him he couldn't come into my room, I could almost see the disappointment on his face.

"Why?" he wanted to know. All he wanted to do was give me this

gift. I recalled the parable of Jesus rebuking his disciples saying let the children come to me, and as much as I wanted to see him, I knew I could not. It was too dangerous.

Though disappointed he asked a simple favor.

> *"Could you give Kim this flower for me? I made it just for her!"* came the little voice.

> *"Of course I will,"* responded my mother's voice thanking him for being so nice and making such a wonderful gift.

Now I have seen the beautiful gardens of France, the gorgeous buds blooming in Switzerland, the most beautiful red roses I've imagined from my husband on the day of our wedding and many, many more. But never have I seen a single flower more beautiful than the one that little boy had made me. The green stem reached out longing for the bright orange flower blooming atop the stem. And this simple flower, made of nothing but pipe cleaners, was the most elegant present I've seen. It was artfully made by a five-year-old boy, and his only desire that day was to give me a gift from his heart.

FAMILY FIRST

My sister is a take-charge kind of person. Her love for people runs deep and her outgoing personality reflects that. She dreams big and follows through. When others, like me, overanalyze and create self-doubt, Valerie jumps in head first and always succeeds! Valerie was living in Chicago at the time of my accident. After she tried to contact my parents, she paced the floor at her boyfriend's apartment in Chicago, debating the best thing to do. After twenty minutes of pacing, she decided she wasn't just going to sit around and wait, so she and Nathan jumped in the car and headed for Iowa. This was a huge sacrifice for Nathan, who would one day become my brother-in-law. The following day was his first day of law school.

Valerie and Nathan had been together for years. They met in college and were sweethearts throughout with a few bumps in the road like most young couples. But even after a spat or two it seemed they should be paired for life. He was intellectual and sharp as a whip, she was fun-loving and analytical as well. Similar to Chad and I, he made her think and she made him fun. They had arrived in Chicago to get him started in law school at Northwestern when they got the call.

"Kim's been in an accident."

Now I'm pretty sure that my soon-to-be brother-in-law was not anticipating a trip outside of the comforts of his newfound apartment when he thought of the weekend before his law school education would begin. But that's exactly where he found himself. With a serious girlfriend pacing the floor knowing her sister had been in a life-threatening accident and that she could not be six hours away and feel good about it. So she paced for a couple of hours and then hurriedly gave him an option…

"I'm going," she emphatically stated. *"I can't just sit here. Are you coming with me or am I going myself?"* With little thought he said, *"I'm coming."*

Nathan had been an usher in our wedding and it was at our reception they had reconnected for what was to be life. Chad and Nathan were tight, having lived together at one point, and my guess is he wouldn't have felt right about staying to go to school. Knowing that my brother-in-law had worked his entire life to earn outstanding grades and be accepted into one of the most prestigious law schools in the country, Northwestern, was impressive enough. But to know that in a moment, he left town the day before classes started takes my breath away. Only a truly genuine, selfless person risks his future for another. His friends contacted the instructors and explained the situation, and they were very understanding. Nathan, being the whiz he is, had no problem catching up.

5

Gut Check Reactions

I never paid much attention to how I looked. It may seem odd that a young woman of 25, whose job was to "look good" on camera never really paid much attention to how she looked. But it was true. I always thought that if what I had to say was accurate, reflective, concise and well communicated, then I "looked good."

I rarely saw the benefit of putting on too much make-up. It just got everywhere, my phone, my clothes. I figured if I followed my taste in clothing, which was very traditional, my clothes would not go out of style and I could make great use of them. My looks just really weren't something I thought about much.

That all changed the day I looked in the mirror for the first time after the accident.

The nurses made a big deal of it. I remember Brenda, my nurse and friend, very gently handing me the mirror and not asking, but rather telling me it was time to look in the mirror. I believe Chad was in the room at the time. I found this odd and think I hastily took it from her hands assuming this was just another task I needed to check off my list before I was allowed to go home. I should've made note of her gentle hands.

When I raised the mirror to my face, I was horrified at what I saw! The bandages had been removed from my head so I got a full picture of what was before me: A red steak of skin, or lack thereof, outlined my entire right cheek. It journeyed from the top of my right temple and just in front of my ear to my jaw line, making me look like one of those two -faced criminals from Batman. My right eye drooped so that it looked half closed, even though my intent had been to look in the mirror wide-eyed. The top of my right ear was singed and dark purple as if it had just melted into my skin. But my head was the hardest to look at. The right side of my head was a matrix of blood, staples, scabs and antibiotic ointment. A still opened, visible wound ran from as far back on my head as I could see right up through the front of my forehead. Dried blood had accumulated and my shaved head was shiny and moist from the antibiotic ointment meant to protect me from my worst enemy, infection. The staples crisscrossed the surgical incision obviously securing everything under my scalp. I couldn't even conjure a more horrific horror movie character that would have rivaled what I looked like that day. The staples that punctured my scalp were foreign objects meant to hold substantial, foundational structures, not the most precious part of the human body.

It was as if this dam of blood and tissue decided to break out, my brains would fall out with them. I couldn't stand to look anymore, but I couldn't move. In warp speed my memory flashed through decades of fun times captured in still photographs I would no longer be able to see.

I pray that that truly was the lowest point of my life. Darkness truly engulfed me that day and I could feel hope extinguishing as I replayed the vision of what I had seen. Though the mirror had been removed, the terrifying images were seared into my mind as tangible as the scars that covered my body.

I cannot remember if Brenda or my mom had to pry the mirror out of my hand or if it fell to my lap when I could no longer look. What I do know is the reflection staring back at me in the mirror that day was no one I recognized, and I would have to search long and hard to find her again.

In the daylight, reality hit home hard. I immediately realized I had to re-learn everything: how to swallow and talk, how to write and walk. It was like starting life all over again.

I tried my best to do what I was told. Amidst endless visits to draw blood (can anybody tell me why that has to happen before 6 a.m.?), checking for infection, taking my temperature and blood pressure, I tried to be patient. The worst had to be my tracheotomy. A ventilator initially allowed me to breathe those early days when I couldn't on my own, but eventually I underwent a tracheostomy, surgically inserting a tube to allowing me to breathe on my own. In order to keep infection out of my lungs, though, I needed suction treatments that literally made me "cough up a lung." I hated them with a passion, feeling like I would choke to death with every one. But I also knew that along with every other treatment, these treatments brought me one step closer to my new normal…and I longed to be normal again.

Doctors and therapists continued to ponder my future quality of life. The physical things like swallowing and breathing on my own were still in question, but I seemed to be making progress. What they had not yet diagnosed was my mental state. Did I remember my own name? Could I recognize my own husband? Obviously the neighbors weren't sure. And neither was anyone else except me.

My mind seemed as sharp as it had ever been, although clearly that was not entirely true. The meds made me see things that weren't really there and I was slow to recall where I was or comprehend what had happened. Fortunately, I didn't lose a beat with the ones I loved, always recognizing and remembering those who were with me and the places they held in my heart. As I continued to ponder and communicate to no avail, I began to find peace in something I've always believed. God is bigger than those who don't yet have a voice.

This all happened before I could talk. Or sing.

6

Happy Birthday & Hospital Food

A FAMILIAR SONG

The day they took out my trache was a victory in itself. It was Columbus Day, Monday, October 13, 1997, exactly 40 days after my accident, and it was more than a federal holiday to me. Columbus may have discovered the new world this day, but I discovered an even greater treasure…my voice!

I don't mind crowds and an audience is always comforting to me, but today was different. I had earned my reputation as the miracle child of the hospital. Not only had I cleared every hurdle, but in general, soared above and beyond them. Iowa Methodist Medical Center was a teaching hospital so I had seen my share of interns. They would follow along behind my real doctors to witness some dressing change or the results of some surgery. But today was a special day.

Today was the day they would remove my tracheostomy. After a month and a half in the burn unit, I was going to speak my first words.

Apparently, it was a banner day for the med students too. My corner room, the luxury suite, with wide, open windows overlooking the medical campus was fairly roomy. Today it was jam-packed. My mother stood to my left holding my hand as she often did. Dr. Reece was to my right with a nurse standing guard. She was armed with the gauze and bandages that accompanied me wherever I went. Then there were faces too numerous to count lining my room. They stood at the foot of my bed, propped up against the windows, and were still streaming in the doorway for just a peek. Perhaps they would hear a whisper or a word that might come out of my mouth at the very moment I was told I could speak again. I remember the sharp tug and release of the tube stuffed down my throat. I squeezed my mother's hand, as was customary with these non-medicated procedures. I coughed a lot. And then my mind goes blank.

Whether or not I said something profound, I have no memory. The occasion obviously called for something profound, funny or inspirational to come out of my mouth. I hope I said "Thank you." But as was typical for these early days in the hospital, my memory is fuzzy when it comes to details. What I do know is one day later, after practicing some very squeaky and poor renditions with my "new" old voice, I sang to my brother.

> "(breath) Hap (pause…cough) hap-py
> Birth (swallow) day (cough) to you.
> Hap-py Birth-day Dear Randy…"

The simple song was far from even good. It was strained, quiet, off key, and dotted with inconsistent breath and coughing. For someone who had sung in choirs from a very young age, had sung in high school musicals and for friend's weddings, it was far from even being average. Honestly, as an outsider, I would have been covering my ears and wondering why anyone would ask this person to sing in public. It was also the best rendition of "Happy Birthday" I had ever sung...or would ever sing.

POTTY TRAINING

I was a twenty-six year old newlywed when I returned to potty training. One of the most degrading tasks of the day was allowing someone, usually my husband or mother to help me to the toilet. Occasionally I would seek the help of a nurse if I was truly desperate. It was exhausting. By this time, I weighed all of 95 pounds soaking wet, but pulling my body out of bed was almost enough to make me wish for the catheter again. I summoned strong hands on both sides to support me, walked about five steps to the restroom and sat relieved just to catch my breath. My assistant stood by to make sure I didn't fall while I used the restroom.

I don't consider myself a vain person, but I am modest and a huge fan of privacy. So sharing my bathroom habits with anyone was not an easy emotional task at all. My mom's nursing training and amazing bedside manner had returned in heartbeat as she fiercely watched over my every need. She was the voice I didn't have as I began my recovery. I was far from the first person she had helped to the bathroom and I wouldn't be the last, but it was still difficult to know I needed help for the most basic of tasks.

Chad, however, was new to this whole caregiver scene, and I was not happy that I was the one bringing him into this world just months after we were married. I had diligently studied our wedding vows and meant every word of standing beside Chad in sickness and health, but this almost sent me over the edge. In my mind, I was asking too much of him. Yet he never once flinched, thought twice or hesitated to be the strong shoulder, literally, that I needed just to do something as simple as get to the bathroom.

JUST ONE BITE

I desperately wanted a Dr. Pepper. It's been my drink of choice, I suppose, since my mother first let me have one. Instead, I ate thick, ice creamy protein shakes as the nurses re-taught me how to swallow. I don't even like ice cream. I progressed quickly through that test only to be told, "No skim milk…it's too thin and you could choke. Only whole milk for a while." While these were mild setbacks, they seemed highly unfair to me. I was getting better after all, right?

But the frustration I felt over not having the beverage of my choice didn't touch my angst when it came to the menu. The menu I was assigned was labeled "soft palette" and it meant "goop." I ate applesauce, creamy soups, Jell-O, and what quickly became the worst of all, mashed potatoes. I was allowed only foods thick enough to re-train my esophagus without allowing me to choke if I wasn't able to swallow. No salad, pizza or nachos for me, although an occasional french fry was smuggled in.

I'm not a patient person, but I am a compliant person most of the time. And what choice did I have? I rationalized. I hadn't lived through all of the initial accident and complications to then die from choking on a bite of hamburger.

Red Jell-O may have been the gourmet food of my early cuisine and since a stomach tube still delivered a majority of the nutrients I needed, "real food" was off limits for a while. When I had sufficiently proven to the nursing staff that I could once again swallow, pizza parties became the highlight. I was a newlywed who desperately wanted a little time with my husband. Holding hands with Chad felt like going on a date, a gentle kiss reminded me of our honeymoon, but the best times that we had together those early days were when we locked the doors, kept everyone out, he crawled into my medical bed and we watched a Husker game.

Chad and I both graduated from the University of Nebraska- Lincoln and we are huge sports fans. When we could talk football and cheer on our team for three straight hours without the interruption of nurses, doctors or therapists, we were newlyweds again. It was as if we were transported back to our college apartments, just hanging out watching a game letting the day pass without a care beyond whether or not the Huskers would win the game.

Eventually we felt generous enough to include family and friends into our football parties. Once I was even allowed to ride down the elevator in a wheelchair out of my room to take command of a waiting room TV for a change of scenery and football.

Pizza parties then became the post-surgical routine. My Dad would often feed the entire nursing staff to celebrate one more successful surgery. There is not a man out there who could rival the generosity of my Dad. A hard worker from the get go, he grew up in San Antonio, Texas, the son of a Southern Pacific railroader. After college my dad was an officer in the army, served in Vietnam and came back to work for the railroad himself, first Missouri Pacific, eventually merging to become Union Pacific. My dad loved people and could make friends with anyone, at the grocery store or at the beach. He was forever taking care of the people who worked for him.

My accident had rocked his world and caused him to reflect on his faith and belief more than at any other time in his life. But in the midst of the hardest times, my Dad did what he always did best, he built relationships. He knew the nurses, their families, other patients and their families, and the people who would eventually come to walk us through the legal process when it came time to make sure it didn't happen to someone again.

Surgeries would become the norm for the foreseeable future, meaning years, and I would get to know the staff of Iowa Methodist Medical Center well. It's amazing the sheer number of people you meet to prep you for a day of surgery. There are receptionists that check you in during the wee hours of the morning and wrap a plastic id badge on your hand, ensuring that in the hours to come when you once again have no voice, doctors and nurses will easily be able to identify you and any allergies in case of an emergency. I always wondered why they were coated in plastic, but after I thought about it for a minute realized that things could get messy in surgery. Thankfully I was consistently spared that picture.

There are nurses who bring you your lovely hospital gown and direct you how to change clothes and where to place your belongings during surgery. Others who transfer you to a rolling bed to wheel you down the hallway and into the pre-op room. There you were handed off to IV nurses, introduced to your anesthesiologist and have a pleasant conversation with your surgeon for last minute questions all before kissing your loved ones goodbye. Techs wheel you into the operating room where another team of nurses and techs are prepping the surgical tools and you for the actual surgery. An army of medical professionals have already assisted you in every detail of your day… and if it's a long surgery, it's often only 7 a.m.

7

Rigorous Routine

THERAPY

Talking opened up a whole new world of therapists to me. I now added three to my daily regimen of baths, eating and healing. Physical therapy, speech therapy and occupational therapy were now part of my rigorous schedule. Physical therapy began with the basics. Turning my head so that my newly placed scalp formed from a muscle in my back would not tighten. I did want to move my head. Sitting on the side of my bed by myself and walking to the bathroom with just a walker quickly grew to laps around the burn unit. I eventually would travel outside of the burn unit for physical therapy.

Here, in the modified gym, designed to baby step all of the patients back to some sense of normal, I felt most at home. Exercise has been a steady, if on again, off again, partner all of my life. I love to work out, breathe fresh air, feel like my body is working the way it's supposed to. I benefit from the way my brain feels quicker, and sharper when I consistently find myself on a quick run or in a class.

When I found myself falling victim to the freshman 15 in college, I found the rec center and plugged in my headphones to find great music and work out until I was dripping with sweat. I didn't do it to compare myself to anyone else, but because I just felt better when my body felt better and it worked off the stress of the day.

When my body seemed to have completely given out on me from literally the top of my head to the tips of my toes, I had to fight back. A full month in a medically induced coma had depleted any muscle tone I had to nothing. I had dropped at least 35 pounds and was sitting below 100 pounds of total weight for the first time since junior high. Strength was a non-existent entity to me now. Surgeries and the respective healing time had zapped every ounce of energy, and every ounce of nutrition I was able to swallow went directly to heal my severely burned body and the remnant wounds from the many surgeries I was having.

The day they first wheeled me into the Physical Therapy (PT) room, it was a familiar place to me. I was no longer held captive in a sanitized hospital room. I had entered a place to work, to sweat and to regain some control over my care and rebuilding my body and strength. This felt normal. Of course this gym was slightly different in composition. I began with the parallel bars that bore my weight while I reprogrammed my legs to walk again. Riding a stationary bike to stretch my knee, lifting weights to rebuild muscle and increasing stamina felt like progress. I was often saddened to see others who would resist their physical therapy. To me it was my ticket out of there so I worked hard. I trained, for me, as if I was an Olympic athlete and I left it all on the table, every hour.

I'm a competitive person by nature and it was more than frustrating to feel like I had so quickly transformed from a young, semi-athletic 26-year-old to a virtual infant in every way. It was heartbreaking to me to know that although my mind, thankfully, was as sharp as it had ever been, I traveled a full lifetime down my body from an 8 month old to an

80 year old. I was relearning to program my brain with basic functionality. I re-learned how to swallow solid foods as if it was my first taste, and I needed to be shown how to hold a pencil as if I was in pre-school. My atrophied muscles were so bad that bearing weight on my legs took me back to the days of puberty when my legs and arms grew so fast that my coordination couldn't catch up. The stamina I had, though, to me resembled more of an 80-year-old, collapsed on the couch, or in this case into my hospital bed and falling asleep before my head hit the pillow.

I mentioned I'm not a patient person. In one fell swoop, I became a toddler in ability, but my mind remained sharp. This was hard. The basic tasks I was charged with were rudimentary and insulting. But it was part of the process and I needed it. So I turned my frustration to smiles and tried to remember how hard everyone was working to get me out of there.

If the gym was where I was most at home, speech therapy meant the other end of the spectrum. The view in the mirror was devastating enough, but for a journalist, who used her mouth for a living, to realize the words I was trying to form wouldn't come out, seemed monumentally unfair. I tolerated exercises to relearn to move my mouth, my jaw and to reform my bite. Speech included relearning how to pronounce basic syllables any kindergartener learns. I tolerated the hours of watching myself in a mirror sounding out words. I tried desperately to make my mouth move in symmetry like it used to. And it was humbling to know that just because cognitively I wanted something, my body was not able to perform it.

This made occupational therapy even more frustrating for me. It began with stale questions. Where are you? Who is the president? How old are you? I heard these repetitious questions urgently every day, sometimes more, until I got bored. Often I wondered what would happen if I answered Abraham Lincoln. Would they whisk me away? But I played along with the game.

I did puzzles and finger exercises and tests with the psychiatrist, where often I found myself saying, "If the only thing wrong with me is that I cannot say the alphabet backwards, I think I'm good. I couldn't do that before the accident."

But where I truly realized my blessings was in group therapy. I was opposed to going from Day One. I had made major progress on my own flying through any tests they set before me at record pace. I was trying desperately to get back to normal…or my "new normal" and I didn't see the point in talking to strangers at all.

I worked so hard to move forward and not look back and was convinced that this group therapy was going to be a leash that pulled me back to the horrible parts of what had happened. I didn't want to relive the pain, the what-ifs, the loss.

I felt like I had navigated those pretty well. I had a faith that was moving mountains, not by me, but the One who saved me from the beginning. And even though tears flowed freely the first time I looked into a mirror, I was determined that I had been given a gift more precious than any obstacle that could come my way.

If ever I needed perspective, God gave it to me in group therapy. While there was much of my situation to lament, there I found myself surrounded by those injured to a greater degree than myself. It was here where I learned to rise above my frustration, difficulty, impossibility to find the blessings no matter how hidden they are.

My true attitude was, why in the world did they think I would want to sit in a room full of strangers lamenting what could have/should have been? That was easy…I didn't. But they told me to do it and so I did. Although this may have been the "worst" part of the hospital emotionally for me, I sat in a room full of traumatic brain injured people and felt sad.

I felt sad that some of them were so lost. I felt sad that some of them were so rude. I felt sad that it was obvious that some would never again be able to function in society in any sense of normal. And I felt sad, that I had been lumped together with this group. I became even more determined to prove them wrong! They were still trying to determine who I was and how different I was from before.

The damage to my head was significant and literally, the miracle of modern medicine combined with answered prayer, saved my life. When my head hit the electrified van, it caused significant damage. Years later I would visually see how much of my brain had been compressed inside of my skull, leaving me with significant spatial impairment and slight loss of mobility on my left side.

It was here that I realized how incredibly blessed I was to have come so far in such a short time. Most people do not survive my injuries. It's the reason the first EMT's on the scene walked on by. But by the grace of God, He decided I had more to do. I could have, should have by all scientific study, sustained egregious permanent injuries that could have taken away my memory, speech, physical abilities and so much more, truly I experienced a miracle.

But others in the room with me, did not. And it was apparent to me from that first day in therapy how blessed I was.

8

Suffocating Dreams

I had conquered many demons in the hospital, or so I felt; physical exhaustion that left me with literally no strength, excruciating pain that would eventually shutter my body into sleep only to jolt me awake hours or minutes later. Haunting days of trying to remember what had happened and where I was. Devastating dreams that were so real to me, I would awake screaming.

I dreamed that my hospital room had a drive-thru of sorts, where people were constantly closing in on me and trying to hurt me. It felt like the worst horror movie I can imagine as I pictured the reality of strangers all but attacking me with everything from swords to knives and hammers.

I know these were the product of a myriad of drugs initially meant to keep me within the drug-induced coma so that my most severe injuries could heal. But as I gained consciousness and my brain began to heal and put together the pieces of what had happened, the nightmares became more vivid, more real, more frightening. I was still unable to effectively communicate what they felt like, or even explain what seemed so real, still unable to talk for the most part, but my family was attuned to my every instinct and they knew that I was visibly upset. Even as Chad and my sister had deduced the fear of the balloons, my mom recognized that I cringed when a large male nurse came near me, and she stood guard diligently by my side when he watched over me on the weekends. I was in and out of clear thought in those early days. The nurse had never done anything but try to help me. He only worked the weekends with me. He was unfamiliar to me and in the darkness of night when he inevitably checked on me, looked even more scary.

My family, especially my mom, did their very best to calm me, though often I could not verbalize the reality of the fear that grabbed hold of me. She would gently repeat that I had been in an accident, where I was, and the names of the people taking care of me.

It is truly a gift of patience that I have never witnessed in anyone else on this earth that my mom had. My mom had the patience of Job.

The reality of the balloons closing in on me had been temporarily removed with the joyful arrival of many Mylar bouquets to the children of the neighboring hospital unit, but the fears and the nightmares didn't cease.

IV's

I'm quite sure my drug-induced coma mixed with true environmental realities combined to form the erratic nightmares I found at my door with every close of my eyes.

One time I dreamed that I was in a room full of patients, all lined up along the walled off room receiving medication through IV's. In my foggy state they appeared as huge football players clearly able to dominate me in size and I dreamed they were trying to steal my medication.

Why I would've perceived them as football players I don't know, although I'm quite sure many of Chad's visits included the TV on and more than a few plays of the latest Husker football game. I also received multiple blood transfusions in the hospital so I suppose it's not a stretch to think that as blood and medication were flowing into my arms, my brain concocted a fear of someone stealing the lifeblood of what I need to survive away from me. I fought them off.

Another nightmare as real to me as the events of the day included me being chased through a myriad of tall white stone pillars. The chase went on as I wove my away through this ancient stadium of sorts, but as I ran behind one on the pillars I found myself standing face to face with the only picture I have ever seen of Jesus.

A man stood dressed in white with the most kind, translucent, crystal clear blue eyes I've eve seen. Time stood still and he asked one question of me, *"Do you believe?"*

Without hesitations I responded, *"I have always believed in you,"* and He was gone.

A song that has resonated with me for years now is written by Mercy Me entitled, "What will it be like?" it never fails to bring tears to my eyes as their phenomenal tenor voices sing,

> *"...Surrounded by Your glory, what will my heart feel*
>
> *Will I dance for you Jesus or in awe of you be still*
>
> *Will I stand in your presence or to my knees will I fall*

Will I sing hallelujah, will I be able to speak at all

I can only imagine…"

"I Can Only Imagine," album: "Almost There" (2002) Mercy Me

I'm convinced that because of the many blessings I have received in my life, the next time I see Jesus, I will fall to my knees with tears streaming from my eyes, unable to find words to say thank you. I can only imagine that it will be understood when I will fail to find words in Heaven if only I can remember the words I already said to Him," I have always believed in you."

But the most startling nightmare I had held total mystique for me until nearly 15 years later. I dreamed that I was in the middle of a bustling third world marketplace. It was dark and crowded with strangers in foreign costumes and at every booth these strangers were shouting for me to stop and hear what they we're saying. But I was not listening...I was desperately trying to catch Chad. He was just ahead of me and quickly disappearing into the crowd with every step. I would catch a glimpse of him and run desperately toward him, longing to be in his presence, but I couldn't catch him. I would run screaming his name and begging him to turn around and hear me, but it was always as if he was just out of earshot and beyond my reach. As the voices of the strangers grew louder and seemed to close in on me, I grew more desperate to catch him.

This was the dream that haunted me the most. Having just married my best friend and planning to spend the rest of my life with him, the thought that he would travel on without me, without even knowing I was here, though I desperately wanted him to see me, was so impossible to comprehend.

The thought of moving forward without him terrified me more than any physical disability I would have to overcome. And for years I would battle with how unfair it was to start our marriage off with such an obstacle to overcome.

Fifteen years later, I was reading a book written by a burn victim and survivor of 911. As I neared the end of the book, I read something that made my heart stop. Halfway across the country, years after my accident, she described the very scene from my dream that I had buried so deeply in my heart and had never spoken of. The marketplace she describes eerily resembles my exact memories and yet while my dream seemed to fade into that marketplace, hers continues on into a dark place I hope never to witness.

Sometime after I read that same description, it dawned on me that God can teach us His lessons even in our dreams. Chad was not the one who would get me through the next five years of surgery. He couldn't save me from the pain, he couldn't relieve me of anxiety, and as much as I wanted him to understand, there was no way for him to possibly comprehend all that I was going through. He couldn't hear my heart. No one could but God. I think that dream told me everything I would need to know for the rest of my life about faith.

It's beyond human comprehension to understand the full complexities of believing in something you can never touch, see or feel. I believe that's why I was trying desperately to chase Chad. I could touch him, see him and feel him. I wanted him to get me through this battle. What I think that dream taught me was that he would never be able to do that. Not Chad, not my family, not the wealth of well-meaning friends. I was going to have to battle this demon myself. And the only one who could possibly fully understand was God, who had sent his Son to Hell and back. But that's what faith is. Knowing that something you can't possibly fully comprehend exists and can assist you in times when all others fail. That's what God does for me...He is the one I should be running to...He is the one who is never too busy, He is the one who will always comprehend and understand what others cannot fathom.

All these years later, as Chad and I celebrate our anniversaries and the journey we've traveled together, I can see how our faith has grown individually and as a couple through this accident. And though it began with some common vows, it was solidified in a terrifying nightmare that would take me years to comprehend. Now that is a Silver Lining.

He gives sight to the blind.

ABIDING LOVE

If I thought the nightmares were a place of darkness and torture to me, I would later find out that they caused my husband utter distress. A night shortly after I had my accident, Chad was working on no sleep. He was driving back to our lonely one-room apartment, just days before full of the life of newlyweds, now sitting empty, except for a few brief trips to change clothes and perhaps take a quick shower before heading back to the hospital.

The overwhelming odds of my survival in any normal sense broke him. He had been told I may never walk again, talk again, feed myself again or even remember who he was. There was also the very real danger of infection and numerous surgeries and that held very real possibilities of ending my life. It was all too much to handle and he had to pull over to the side of the road.

I'm not sure up until then Chad had even entertained the idea that everything wouldn't be okay. Chad is the most optimistic, can-do person I know, but that was not the reality of those early days. Time inched along as they waited for a sign that I would actually wake up.

There was a natural bounce in his step the day I met Chad. In fact, I often teased him about this, but this good-natured happiness was literally embodied in everything about him, including his walk. After the first day in the hospital where he clarified that I indeed was not dead, I'm quite sure he planned out every methodical step of my re-covery in his mind, assured that things would work out.

Chad, forever the life of the party, played his role well even in the hospital waiting room. Visitors would constantly stop by anxious for any word of my recovery, but there was none to give. Valerie, my sis-ter would later tell me, "You would not have known that we weren't celebrating a full recovery." Chad would break the uncomfortable silence of hearing there was nothing to report over and over again with well-meaning friends, neighbors and strangers.

Though I wasn't there to witness it, this didn't come as a surprise to me at all. Chad has always been the life of the party. He had an ef-fortless away of meeting new people and with minutes, they felt as if they had known him their entire life. He could have a conversation with anyone and at every wedding we ever attended by the end of the night, you would've thought he was the long last son of the family whether we had ever met them before or not.

So the fact that in the awkward situation he now found himself, trying to answer unanswerable questions about the health of his wife, he was able to make everyone feel comfortable didn't surprise me one bit.

Imagine showing up at the hospital to visit and finding out that I had not yet woken up yet. Pretty uncomfortable and disheartening for everyone involved, so Chad was protecting my family the only way he knew how, he took on the role of chief host of the waiting room and put everyone at ease.

But that role can only last so long before the recognition of the gravity of the situation comes crashing down around you. So this night, while he was driving home with an empty seat beside him, it came like an avalanche. He wondered if I would ever wake up again, as recent conversations came to mind. Friends had asked him what he was going to do if I could never talk, walk or remember him again. So much of his life was flashing before him and it finally broke him. So beneath the full moonlight of a star filled sky, hidden in the shadows of the trees, he cried out to the only One in a position to help.

Amidst the privacy of trees and virtual silence my strong, optimistic, amazing husband of three months broke down, finally pleading with God, "Please give me my wife back."

He answered with the peace that surpasses all human understanding. Chad would never break again....

Those prayers were answered in the coming weeks, but even as the victories had mounted over the course of the past few weeks and the celebration should have started, as I was able to leave the hospital and go home, it was only another treacherous journey.

9

Reflections Of Fire

It was a Saturday night and we were coming off the high of competing well in national dance competition in Dallas, Texas years before when I was still in high school. A twelve-hour bus ride home had been exhausting as had the weeks of preparation and although New Year's was right around the corner, what I really wanted to do was just crash at home and recover a little. But my friends Brenda and Michelle concocted the idea of hosting a New Year's party and the entire drill team was likely going to be there. It sounded like fun and all it took was a few words of encouragement from another friend to be all in. How do you pass up a New Year's party after a week of such hard work?

It was like any other high school party. Music thumped against the walls. Half of the house jumped around dancing to the beat while the others played quarters in the garage. There was a crew lined up around the keg, that fixture of these parties I always avoided. I was never a drinker. I didn't like even the smell of beer so why would I waste my time drinking to oblivion? For those who did, the evening ended stumbling around looking like a idiot, espousing grand ideas about the future or rehashing the latest football game. I wasn't interested and especially on this night when I was tired. The music was loud, and the house seemed packed, I made a short appearance, talked with a few friends, thanked my hosts for inviting me and said good night.

Another ordinary party...a new year. We were all juniors or seniors making plans for our future. I had one year yet to go and was trying to decide where I might go to college, pretty sure that journalism was going to be my focus. I fell into bed that night and think I was asleep before my head hit the pillow, thankful for a soft place to fall.

The phone ringing woke me up the next day. Not once or twice, but pretty insistently and often. When my mom called that it was for me I figured it was one of my friends calling to make plans for the day or share some funny story about what happened last night after I left. I could not have been less prepared for what I heard next.

"Kim, there's been an accident," came the distorted voice on the other end of the line. *"There was a fire last night at Brenda's house* (the same house I had been in just hours before). *Four people are dead. Brenda, Michelle and Brenda's brother and nephew were killed."*

I was struck speechless, not something that happened often, and as I choked out my response, and heard the voice telling me we were all meeting at someone's house to be together, I struggled to comprehend what I had just been told. Two of my friends were dead in the house I had been in just hours before.

Brenda? Michelle? Dead? This couldn't be...I had just spent a week with them in Dallas. We were dancing, laughing and busy comparing how cool our uniforms were. Now that not so distant memory seemed so trivial I almost threw up. In an instant, their lives were gone. No graduation, no plans for the future, no life, plain and simple.

As I hung up the phone on my bedside table I began to cry. I glanced at my Bible sitting there and wondered aloud, "Why?" There were no answers, although the cause would later be traced to cigarettes that were never put out. But the question hung with me like a damp cloud...waiting for the raindrops to fall. Why? And so I picked up the book that I had read so sporadically and randomly opened it to page that gave me the answer I needed to hear.

> "No temptation has seized you but that which is common to man. And take heart because God is faithful. He will not let you be tempted beyond what you can bear. But when you are tempted He will give you strength to find a way out."
>
> 1 Corinthians 10:13

In the counseling that followed with the drill team and school, through meetings with her distraught mother, and through the funeral I was strangely comforted knowing that someone else was in charge. But it didn't squelch the pain.

For months, I would drive by the house and just stare at the burnt remains. I was struck not only by the damage, but by the total destruction. The haunting of the screams the burning rafters must've heard that night. How absolute terror must have gripped them when they realized they wouldn't be able to get out. How the fire must have engulfed them. For once in my life I was happy for the presence of beer at the house. To me it was so disturbing that people thought they had to consume alcohol to have a good time, but that next morning and in the weeks to follow I would pray that maybe mercifully they would have drunk enough beer that night that they simply slept through the most painful of deaths. I was struck by the core rocking thought that I had been just hours away from being in that house when it burned to the ground.

It really was a first harsh lesson in how unfair life was. Brenda and Michelle were kind, good-hearted, fun loving girls. And now life had dealt them a final blow...one they couldn't fight back from. They didn't learn a casual lesson or even make a tragic mistake that could affect their life teaching them to make decisions differently the next time. They were gone, never to have another day to say an "I love you," or to make someone smile or laugh. They were dead.

I visited Brenda's mom that first year. I took note of the empty spots on our drill team as we choreographed our new routines, I silently muttered their names at graduation and thought of them daily even after graduation.

I would eventually go to college carrying the weight of what had happened with me just as literally as the books to my first college classes. As a tribute to Brenda and Michelle I hung a sign in my dorm room; another verse that gave me peace.

> "Greater love has no one than this that He lay down His life for his friends."
>
> John 15:13

I was quite sure that would be the most awful of deaths, to be consumed by fire, suffocated by smoke and desperate for air even while the fire burned layers and layers of skin from their very bodies. In my eyes, they had died the most horrific of deaths. They were gone. And the most haunting question that followed me like a shadow for years was why I wasn't. It wasn't the last time I would ask myself that question.

10
Anxious Homecoming

THANKSGIVING

Surgeries were sprinkled in between therapy and they came often. I would just finish from one, return to my routine of therapy and another day in the operating room was scheduled. After a single major surgery any doctor will tell you it will be six to eight weeks before you feel like yourself again. Instead, I had days or occasionally a few weeks to catch my breath before I would do it all over again. In the days after surgeries, I recovered; mainly slept and ate little. After recovery the day's schedule was more rigorous; blood draw, breakfast, physical therapy, bath, lunch, speech therapy, occupational therapy, dinner and bed. Often, I would have to find time to sneak in a nap amidst the crazy schedule. But as days passed and I gained strength, I wanted more and more to leave.

I was anxious to leave the walls of the Burn Unit. While the nursing staff was kind and caring and had become family, the dull walls and endless routine was exhausting. I progressed enough to earn a trip outside once in a while and that respite was thrilling.

The first full outing outside of the Burn Unit I recalled was when friends from Nebraska were visiting. At this early stage, I was still unable to speak, but I distinctly recall the warmth of the sunshine on my bandaged head. Familiar faces swarmed around me, though a few names were slower to recollect. I was extremely frustrated by that until later realized that some of the visitors were friends of my brother or sister whom I had only met once or twice.

Not one to naturally take note of the flowers, the bright yellow and orange hues seemed to leap off of the ground and attack my senses. The bright colors were such a refreshing contrast to the stark off white walls of the hospital room, although my family had done a valiant job of decorating with cards and pictures. The smell of the blooming fall flowers proved so distinct and refreshing they took my breath away, such a nice change from the medicinal hallways of the Burn Unit and tub room. And birds sang, lifting their voices in the last warm days of fall to make sure everyone knew they were coming back.

And then there were nice familiar friends, kindly lying to me with comments of how good I looked. My ghostly frame, frail and swallowed up by the wheelchair must have been a frightening sight. Soon it was as if we were transported back to college just hanging out once again.

True to form, Chad would engage each member of the crowd as my ears strained to hear every story of normalcy regaled by the group. Chad was sarcastically making jokes of how he had mastered the electronic bed and virtually every other piece of medical equipment housed in the Burn Unit. One look from me, reminding Chad that he had gone too far, told my friends I was still there. It was a look anyone we knew was familiar with...Chad was always the truth exaggerator, I was always the practical truth teller.

A trip four floors down an elevator and wheeled into a tiny courtyard may not seem like much of a trip, but they may as well have transported me to the beaches of the Atlantic or the mountains of Colorado, I was so excited to be outside. That day reminded me of what I was fighting for...freedom, fresh air, God's beauty surrounding me everywhere. In my forced silence, for a short time, I found it that day.

I even earned a pizza party off of the floor so Chad and I could have a date to watch a Husker football game. Neither Chad nor I had grown up in Nebraska. Chad's dad was in the Air Force and traveled from base to base. He started in upstate New York, moved to Michigan, Alaska and eventually landed in Nebraska for college. We had migrated throughout the Midwest, South and East coasts, and as the plan took shape for each of us, I ended up in Nebraska as well.

I was appalled, really, when we first moved to Nebraska, that everyone, and I do mean everyone, cheered for this little known college team, the Cornhuskers. You couldn't even go to the grocery store without having your receipt printed with Go Big Red (GBR). I had lived in cities with multiple professional sports teams all of my life. I was a die-hard St. Louis Cardinals baseball fan, having learned from my Dad to keep book with Ozzie Smith at shortstop and Keith Hernandez on first base. For football, the other sport we watched incessantly growing up, the Dallas Cowboys were my NFL team and the Texas Longhorns were my college team.

My Dad was a University of Texas graduate, so really my allegiance was always to Texas teams, until I became a Husker. In college my burnt orange blood turned distinctively red. Chad and I became Huskers not only as card carrying students, but in spirit as well. It was a great time to be a Husker with a National Championship the year of graduation and friends on the Homecoming Court. Our college memories solidified on Saturday afternoons. So even after we both graduated, Husker football was a part of our Saturday routine.

After my accident, we had very little routine when it came to our lives as a married couple. So in the hospital, when I had little control over what tomorrow would hold, a Husker game could transport me back to a time when we could once again be a couple out on a date.

That was the one time I absolutely refused any nursing staff in the room. After 24 hours, 7 days a week of on-call nurses, doctors and other assorted staff intruding any moment they wanted to, I was ready for some privacy. Ready for the med students to find someone else to attend to.

I told Dr. Reece in no uncertain terms that I was out of there by Thanksgiving! He took me at my word and I worked hard to meet their expectations. They worked alongside me, pushing me at every opportunity.

I worked hard to relearn the basics. I was eating pizza instead of mashed potatoes. I had graduated to skim milk and was gaining a little weight slowly, but surely. I knew the road ahead would be fraught with obstacles and years of surgery, but "going home" sounded so good, so healing and so scary.

LEAVING

In the days before my release, my view became crowded with the one thing I didn't want to see. Remote live trucks. By this time I was beginning to see the big picture of how my accident developed, and the one thing I did not want to see, but yet seemed captivated by, was television remote live trucks. They swarmed the front of the hospital.

The story of the day had passed me by two months earlier. Now the reporters inquiring about my daily progress, the requests for interviews and certainly the live trucks parked outside the hospital on my behalf were a not-so-distant memory. The hospital had been a fierce protector of my privacy and there had been much talk about how I would be able to leave out of the back door to avoid any lingering reporters anxious for a first look at me. I was pretty sure the live trucks that now encircled the hospital were not interested in me anymore, but somehow, just the sight of them made me nervous.

I came to find out that Iowa Methodist Medical Center was no longer concerning themselves with my story, much to my relief, but another medical miracle was to take place and had diverted the attention of the throng of med students…the Septuplets were about to be born.

November 19, 1997, the world's first set of septuplets to survive infancy arrived at Iowa Methodist Medical Center, the same hospital I was recovering in. Born nine weeks early, the McCaughey septuplets were from Carlisle, Iowa. When the couple discovered they were carrying 7 babies, they declined selective reduction, saying they would, "put it in God's hands." All seven of them survived. Clearly God's plan had carried them through.

On one of my many elevator rides to and from therapy, my mom and I shared the space with seven tiny incubators, set to house the largest group of babies born to a single mom in over a decade. The fact that this was the occasion for the live trucks seemed to ease my fear of seeing the very truck responsible for my accident. Seven tiny babies was definitely a newsworthy story and I was proud of my profession for rallying around what everyone hoped would be a wonderful, positive story; the story of new life.

I'm not sure how many loads of stuff Chad and my dad had to take to the cars before I was actually wheeled out, but in 2 ½ months of being there, there was a lot. We brought home cards, stuffed animals, personal items and then there was the medical equipment that would accompany me everywhere for the next several months. I remember thinking as they wheeled me out that I should be allowed to walk out on my own two feet, but that would mean breaking a cardinal hospital rule..."Thou shalt not be discharged without allowing the hospital staff to make you feel sick one last time." A wheelchair ride out of the hospital was not an option. It was mandatory.

And once again there is a reason for that. I remember it taking every ounce of energy I had to get from the wheel chair to the car, something I very much wanted to do.

Months of rehab, years of surgery and battles lay ahead, all presenting their own challenges. While the last months of hourly progress had seemed long, what I was yet to face seemed like the impossible. And on the way home I was gripped with fear.

At no time in my life had I feared anything...I had been nervous, but never afraid to try something new. Now I had conquered all of these demons and so much more, but for whatever reason, riding in the front seat of our car for the first time nearing sundown, I was stricken with absolute panic and fear for what was to come.

I had what I'm sure would be classified as a panic attack. Nothing was safe anymore...not the cars on the road, the speed we were moving, and I was sure there was something lurking just beyond the dense trees of the park we were driving by. The park where Chad had asked for his wife back.

Our Wedding Day, June 28, 1997
(courtesy Regal Photography, 1997)

At WOI-TV5 with sister, Valerie and mom, Judy

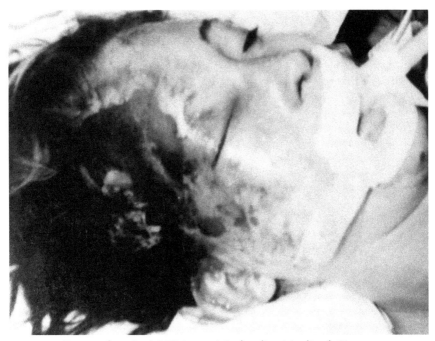

September 3, 1997 Iowa Methodist Medical Center

Brother, Randy and Angie's engagement party

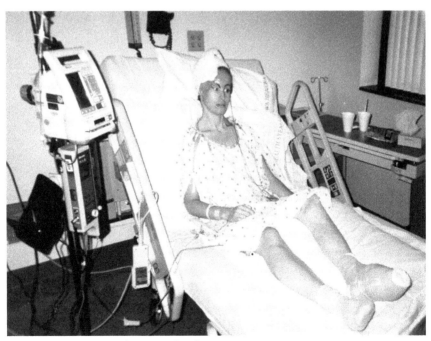

Recovering from multiple surgeries, many yet to come

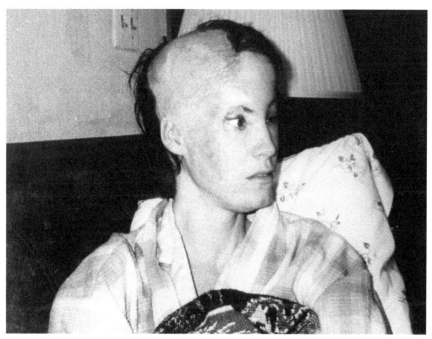

Post surgery for tissue expansion

Kansas City Chiefs game with siblings
Randy & Angie, Chad & Kim, Nathan & Valerie

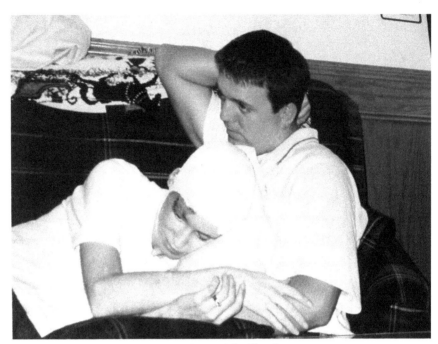

Resting with Chad

Nathan and Valerie's Wedding Day, August 7, 1999
(courtesy Regal Photography, 1999)

The True Silver Lining

Family Picture 2016
Kim, Caleb, Logan, Addison, Chad

11

The Postman
Doesn't Always Ring Twice

DOORBELL

After I transitioned to our one-bedroom apartment, life fell into a bit of a rhythm. Days were mostly spent trying to rest, recoup, gain weight and trying to write an occasional wedding thank you note: the biggest project interrupted because of my accident. Not much excitement, but the daily celebrations of stepping up the speed in walking from the bedroom to the living room.

My return home and to some sense of reality beyond the hospital doors was tough. It may have been encapsulated in one tiny ring of the doorbell for me. Home life was a challenge in our one-bedroom apartment. At the same time, it was so amazingly freeing to not be in a hospital room, trapped by doctors and nurses and that seemed like pure bliss.

I began to realize the blessing of handicap accessible equipment while my mother tried to wrestle a bath chair into our tiny shower.

It was still humbling to know I was too weak to even stand for a few minutes under the trickling water. There is likely no measure of tears my mother shed for me in those first days and months behind closed doors, but God gave her unimaginable peace, and so to me she was always positive, always helpful, always attuned to my every need. The perfect mother, the perfect nurse.

The floors were cleared of excess clutter so that I could maneuver more easily, if not tremendously slowly, first with my walker, then my crutches and finally the cane. I moved at a snail's pace from room to room, the bathroom, bedroom and living room. The square footage was tiny and looking back at the time it took to get from the bed to the couch is almost laughable. What would now take fifteen seconds, quite possibly took about 3 minutes. And that was on a good day. Steps were painful, balance was precarious at best and the sheer energy it took to transport myself 20 feet from one room to the next, is nearly impossible to describe. I remember little activity those days other than sleeping and trying to eat more to gain back all the weight I had lost. And while our couch had once been cluttered with thank you notes for wedding gifts, it now seemed over-run with bandages, gauze, ointments and medical supplies. The thank you's were on hold until I had more strength.

This is my disclaimer to anyone who did not receive a thank you for my wedding. I'll gladly send one now if you let me know. Is 18 years overdue according to Emily Post?

I was adjusting to the little things, but what sticks most clearly in my mind was the difficulty I had looking in the mirror. I had never been a vain person, and I hope I am not to this day, but the anxiety I felt witnessing my own fresh battle scars especially to my face was overwhelming. I could somehow comprehend the injuries to my leg, feet and hip, temporary wounds that would in time heal, but when I looked at my face and my head, I was literally frightened. My own reflection seemed so foreign to me that although I had the freedom to un-bandage my wounds and let them heal and breathe, rarely did I do so.

Except for one day. Chad had gone to work and my mom stepped out. She was our chief household manager, buying groceries, cooking and cleaning, all the while assisting me daily with everything from the bathroom breaks to meals. My guess is that she was either at the grocery store or the post office. And this day I was tired. Happy, but tired. My burned leg was unwrapped, my scarf was off and as I recall I was contemplating those thank you notes when the doorbell rang. I went nowhere fast. So without thinking I grabbed my cane and plodded to the door, pretty sure that no one was going to assume anyone was home by the sheer time it was taking me to move the five steps from the couch to the front door.

But when I flung open the door, smile on my face ready to greet a visitor, the postman about fell over.

In that spilt second I realized I had not covered my head or my leg and I must be a piece of work to look at. He stammered something and I stammered something back and he fled as if he were the lead character in a horror movie and aliens had just invaded the planet.

I think Chad and I shared a good laugh about it that night, but in reality it stung. No one had ever run from me when I came bearing a smile and the reality of how everyone else would now see me truly began to sink in. In the hospital I was a medical miracle, a testimony for each and every person who dedicated themselves to helping patients over the years. To the outside world, and especially to strangers, I was a monster. It was that reality that kept haunting me over and over. This time it came crashing down in the ring of a doorbell.

12

The Story Not The Storyteller

TV COVERAGE

While I was still in the hospital, in between my intense rehabilita-
tion, I would return to the burn unit room to rest. As I gained strength
it became increasingly difficult to pass the time in the hospital, so I
would flip channels on the TV. I was recovering from one of countless surgeries when there on the TV screen were pictures of me at the
accident sight. I was being carted off in an ambulance the day of my
accident. Though you could not see my face from the angle of the
camera shot, my lifeless arm hung down from the EMTs strong arms
as they carried me into the ambulance to try and save my life. It was
a surreal moment for me. Months later the story was still all over the
news I learned that day. It appeared on every news channel, on the
radio and the slightest updates would be written up in the paper.
When David, my colleague, was released from the hospital; my being
upgraded to fair condition it seemed to go on and on, none of which
I had seen until that day. My family had become extremely protective
of my privacy, understandably, since everyone from the elementary
school to the Governor's office wanted to know how I was doing.

I vaguely remember my mother telling me that someone wanted to come and visit me in the hospital and say thank you for coming to David's aid and saving his life. It may have been the Governor or a City Councilman, and she had told them no. I remember questioning whether or not that was an ethical move on our part. It seemed a bit disingenuous to have spent the last years of my life asking people daily to allow me to put them on the news, but when the tables were turned I refused...or my family did for me. But there would be a time and place for that, and it was the right decision. I'm not even convinced I fully understood what had happened to me at that point and I was in far too weak a physical state to undertake that.

I did have one visitor I distinctly remember. My family had told me that David Bingham, my colleague who I had been working with that day, wanted to come and see me. I didn't think a thing of it. I had had many familiar faces come and visit, both family and friends, and of course, I considered Dave a friend too. If I remember right, he and his wife, Kim, came into my room that day. It's a fuzzy recollection, other than I remember his arm was bandaged up and in a sling with what was left of his burned fingers hanging out.

There seemed to be an unspoken tension in the room that day, although I couldn't put my finger on it. As he and Kim stood there in my room I felt small. He was strong enough to walk into the room and I was happy for him that he was doing so well, but I was still relegated to a wheelchair. Should I have been upset? Here standing in my room was the man who had first raised the mast into the live wires and we were both injured because of it, but instead of anger I just felt peace. Peace that we were both on the road to recovery and bonded forever. Was I supposed to be angry? Was I supposed to yell and scream? Was I supposed to burst into tears? None of that happened as I recall. I'm not even sure what the conversation was like other than pleasant and how was he doing? Would he be going back to work? It seemed like an every day, "Haven't seen you in a while" conversation to me, but I wonder what the rest of the room felt.

DOCUMENTED JOURNEY

One day the phone rang with a call from a college acquaintance who happened to be a reporter for the Omaha World Herald, back in Nebraska. Rainbow Rowell and I knew each other from a few journalism classes, although she went the print route while I headed for broadcasting.

Rowell is a brilliantly creative writer, so very funny, incredibly talented and genuine. She called asking if she could come with a photographer and do a follow up story to my accident. I quickly agreed, still feeling badly that I had turned away so many requests earlier in my recovery. I was still a journalist at heart.

She was kind and compassionate in her interview and since my sister happened to be in town, the photographer took a nice picture of us together. I wore a denim hat, one that would sit beside the couch for the foreseeable future in case the postman ever came back.

I remember being struck by how different I looked in that picture, but quickly went on to read the article. At the time it seemed like another one of Rainbow's articles, and I read it just as I would have been critiquing one of our J-school homework assignments.

But this was before my friend Julie came to visit. TV was different, as I would soon find out.

TELEVISED PROGRESS

Julie was probably my closest friend at the station back at KLKN-TV8 in Lincoln. I had many co-workers I considered dear friends, actually not many I didn't, but Julie and I saw the world through a similar lens, so there were few daytime reporters I would have trusted my story to more than her.

She came to interview me and the conversation flowed easily. We talked of what I remembered about the accident (not much) and how my recovery was going. I spread out legions of cards and gifts sent to me so she could have enough B-roll to cover my words. I shoddily played the piano for her, knowing that me sitting in a chair wasn't going to be enough to cover the story, still fully recognizing how Julie would need to produce this story. The action of trying to play the piano was both therapy and good visually for television. I had done this same drill a million times. Listening to the person you were interviewing while silently scanning the room for pictures that would match the words or listening for an obscure answer to keep the interest of the viewer. I was a happy participant and wanted to make it easy on Julie and really I had nothing to do that day other than spend time with my dear friend.

Julie would send me copies of the stories weeks later and I remember being excited to see her work, at first. I popped in the tape and watched the stories as my mind numbed. What had been a relaxing and encouraging time with a friend just weeks ago had now become a documented account of all that I had lost. I stared at that unfamiliar face on the screen and wondered what I was thinking, going on camera looking like that.

It had been months since my accident and I felt better each day, but these videos for me were about something so vastly different. They represented my world crashing down before me. I had forever been driven in my career goals and whatever I did I did 200%. That effort usually paid off. I was a good student, successful in extracurricular activities, had managed to make wonderful fiends and most especially had believed that whatever I wanted to accomplish I could if I worked hard enough. In those four minutes of video, Julie had done a fantastic job of telling my story and had woven my words beautifully into a moving story of my recent life for everyone else to hear. I for the first time though, wondered if I would ever live a normal life again. It seemed unlikely that I would be able to return to the career I loved, and as I stared at the shell of a person with half a face, I sunk into sadness.

13
Refined By Fire

I had lived through the most dangerous part of the initial accident; blood clots on my brain, infections that threatened to derail my fight, surgeries that literally dismantled my body and put me back together again. These were the earliest of days when my life was still, by all counts, in jeopardy, but though I still held a lot inside, some of the most difficult injuries I would face were the ones visible to all the world.

The burns to my face were dramatic and although my first thought was always how thankful I was just to be alive, the first time I looked in a mirror was an overwhelming and excruciating experience. I could still remember vividly. Staples literally held my head together, a crisscross of stitches that seemed alien in all counts of the word. That initial shock was revisited every time I crossed paths with a mirror.

Burns had exposed my face in such a way that I wondered if even the most masterful hands would be able to craft a "normal" looking face again. I no longer looked anything like the Kim I remembered and I wondered what I looked like to my husband of two months and the family that had looked out for me for 25 years.

Pressure garments for burn victims are standard issue in order to minimize the scarring and heal skin with less deformity. Burned skin, at least on my leg, looks like those models of the human brain, woven with bumpy paths, it rises and falls in certain areas and is stretched tight in others. My doctors would secure skin grafts from my healthy skin to help in the healing process, but it was still a patchwork of various textures and less that smooth to the touch. Pressure garments are meant to hold all of that healing or new skin together, minimizing the raised scars. They are literally skintight stockings, custom measured in increments of a millimeters to fit as tightly as possible. Every couple of months, I received new ones in case they had stretched out to the point where you could actually breathe.

In the early days when my leg was still healing, the ONLY way to get them on was to have them outfitted with a full-length zipper. Have you ever tried to put a sleeping bag back into its small case? You have to manipulate the zipper so that no part of the material is caught in the zipper and causes it to break. Picture that with burnt skin.

Any muscle I had once had was atrophied and what was left was healing burnt skin that somehow needed to be sucked into this garment. I now know plenty of burn patients who didn't follow doctor's orders with pressure garments, and I get it. Because I am generally a rule follower, I dutifully zipped myself into these garments, after a slow and energy-draining sitting shower, most often with someone's help. A disruptive thought entered my brain. All those years I had not really cared what I looked like, and now with great emotional pain that part of me was dissolving in the reflection of what I now saw.

14

The Ugly Side Of Progress

EXPANDERS

In January of 1998 Chad and I had moved back to Nebraska and moved in with my parents. I still needed help with everyday tasks like bathing, getting to the bathroom and getting my pressure garments on. My mom's nursing skills once again came in handy as she was a masterful director of healing. She was detailed and organized when it came to managing my multiple medications. Gentle and kind when her 26 year-old daughter needed help bathing and the consummate nutritionist, pushing water to hydrate, proteins and iron to build back muscle and blood supply and rest to help healing.

Eventually, we would move into our own house in Lincoln, just 50 miles down the road. This was a freedom in and of itself. Not just as a young couple buying their first house, but for what it stood for…me being able to care for myself in an entirely new way.

Now that I no longer had to live in the hospital, but just visit, it became a welcome and friendly place. There everyone knew what had happened to me. I didn't need to explain my story, and everyone else had one of their own. It was now the outside world I dreaded.

Of course I was surrounded daily by smiles and warmth and a family thanking God for the miracles we had witnessed, but the casual stranger, and even some casual acquaintances found it hard to hide their shock. I can't blame them. I was a sight to behold. Bandages on my left leg had me looking like a mummy, I had lost so much weight and muscle mass I looked like a skeleton, the scarves on my head couldn't hide the scarring on my face, and my right eye was without half of my eyebrow and drooped half closed leaving me with only partial vision. Let's be real. A smile can only mask so much.

Despite my new found awareness of my devastating looks, I braved it all with my smile. If I was okay with it, surely everyone else would be too, right? It worked well for a while, but day after day, when things are as difficult as they were for me then, is a long time to "wear" a smile.

My hair follicles had been burned off so I could not grow hair on the right side of my head. Enter the amazing surgery called tissue expansion. Basically what was required was the surgical implant of a silicon balloon (or two or three), under my scalp. For the next 8 weeks I would have weekly saline injections to "inflate" the implant. And at the end of the 8 weeks I would have another surgery to remove the implants and stretch the skin or scalp over to secure it to the side of my head. I would then need time to heal from that surgery and we would do it all again, slowly marching my forehead and hair over to the right side of my head. This process lasted several years and it was a hard, daily battle.

This complicated and amazing surgical technique was the one that now allows me to look like I have a full head of hair. It's truly amazing to think about, but it was unsightly to be sure.

Likely, not many of you have witnessed someone with a large tumor-looking thing growing out of her head. There were the typical starrers, people who would not ask, but rather just stare in a shocked kind of way until they realized they were staring and quickly turn away. I always pictured these people a conjuring up all kinds of crazy stories about what had happened to me. Others were bold enough to ask, staring with pity in their eyes as I regurgitated for the umpteenth time the Cliff's Notes version of the story.

TIPPING POINTS

Two years into these surgeries, I was hitting the frustration tipping point. Chad and I had decided to go out to dinner with some friends we had known for many years. It had been a long and painful week of travelling to Des Moines for the last of my inflations before this particular surgery. I was exhausted, grouchy and felt like my head was about to explode. I just wanted to curl up on the couch and wish the surgery was done. But in true Chad fashion, he was having none of it and said, "Grab your purse, we're going out." Thank goodness he regularly did this and didn't let me sit at home wallowing in my sadness. The days before surgery especially seemed to be times when I worried that this might be the one that went wrong and I could quickly dissolve into sadness.

But tonight, I was really looking forward to dinner with our friends, who I knew would regale us with funny stories of life with young boys and would be able to make me laugh. They also knew every detail of my surgical history and knew how hard this week was for me but would do exactly what I needed them to do…not even mention it until the end of the night when they would tell me I was in their prayers.

So we drove across town to the restaurant and walked in to meet them. Just as I sat down, my head started to throb and I knew I needed to take some pain pills before I started eating, but when I reached into my purse a sense of panic hit me. I had taken my last pain pill from my purse and forgotten to fill it up. I knew there was absolutely no way I was getting through dinner without them, being this close to surgery and even skipping one dose would have me in excruciating pain so I said to Chad, *"You stay and order my food...I'll run home and be right back."*

I jumped in the car and as I drove, let my mind wander to my impending surgery. I had two huge inflated implants in my scalp at the time and the beautiful designer scarf my friend, Stephanie had brought me all the way from Italy, was barely able to cover the bulging implants protruding from my head.

I was nearly home when I was stopped at a red light and made the mistake of looking at the car immediately to my right. There sat a car full of four teenage boys, every last one of them staring at my deformed head. At that very moment, before I could look away, all four of them simultaneously burst into laughter and I burst into tears. The light turned green and I quickly turned into a parking lot, letting the tears cascade down my face and sobbing uncontrollably. It had been over two years since my accident and there was no end in sight. I racked my brain for a verse to cry out.

> *"Do you not know, have you not heard, the Lord God is the master of the universe... His understanding no one can fathom."*
>
> *Isaiah 40:28*

I caught my breath and realized I had found His peace again. I made it home, for a moment thought about staying there, but determined not to give into grief, I shoved pain pills in my mouth and purse and headed back to the restaurant, never mentioning the breakdown in the parking lot. That night as planned, Vicodin and our good friends had me laughing once again.

These varied reactions, while pretty common, were hard to take, but never seemed to mitigate the hurt I felt in those long years. I had witnessed incredible insensitivity when it came to people and their reactions to me, but also great kindness.

HONESTY

By far, my favorite reaction was from a little girl in the store one day. This time the process had been extremely tedious and painful and I was grouchy to say the least. Thought it's not really my personality, I was sick of the stares and tempted to tear off my scarf and scream at unsuspecting, staring strangers, *"Is this what you want to see?"* Stores were the worst. I think one day a lady almost tripped over her cart trying to get a look at my head as I walked by. So I was thinking as I stood in the checkout line… *"One more person to see and then I can go home to Chad, I know he'll make me laugh."*

But in front of me stood a mother and her young daughter who looked at me with the biggest eyes I had seen all day. At this point I was again days away from my next surgery in an effort to re-grow my hair and I had a balloon the size of a pear sticking out of my forehead, and another expander the size of an orange on the back of my head so there was no telling how scary I looked to this little girl, even with my scarf trying to cover it up.

But this little angel looked at me and asked simply and honestly, *"What happened to your eye?"*

Moments before I had been ready to tear off someone's head for staring at me, and this sweet little girl didn't notice it at all. The only thing she noticed was that my eye was hurt. This little girl in all her angelic sweetness just wanted to know if my eye was okay. As I smiled and answered that I had been in an accident, but I was okay now, I could see the relief in her eyes and she had reinforced for me a valuable lesson, that the keys to the soul are truly found in the eyes.

Children have always been the best therapy for me. And believe me I've had it all…speech therapy, physical therapy, occupational therapy and group therapy, and yet there's nothing quite like the boldness of a child and their telling questions. The combination of genuine curiosity and cutting honesty is so refreshing and sustaining.

ATTITUDES AND ANESTHESIOLOGISTS

Adults were not always so easy. I was back in Des Moines, for foot surgery this time. By the time I reached this particular surgery, my medical charts were about the size of five full size dictionaries, so an additional person would be assigned to my case just to transfer the mounds of medical records that now defined my recent past. I usually breezed through the first part of the morning until about pre-op time when my anxiety would reach full tilt. You would think since I had done this so many times before it would be basically routine, but though on the outside it may have seemed like old home week for me, I was still terrified inside.

I was a frequent flyer in the OR. Everyone knew me and I know most of the team too, but not today. The only thing that seemed routine today is that I've traveled to the OR with my typical amount of anxiety. It doesn't matter how routine surgery in your life becomes, it NEVER becomes less frightening. But covered in prayer from my family, I went to the pre-Op room with Chad. You were allowed one guest into the pre-Op room and Chad was the lucky one.

We said hello to the familiar faces and I grabbed Chad's hand and demanded that he talk. You see, the very worst part of it all for me was ALWAYS the IV. It hurt. It hurt a lot and it was the first physical pain of what was sure to be weeks and sometimes months of pain-filled recovery.

So I would say to Chad, *"Please just talk to me about the beach, football, anything to get my mind off of this IV and surgery."* My veins were shot by now and I was a "tough stick," which I loudly proclaimed to anyone who came near me with a needle. I wanted their very best effort the first time. But today it wasn't happening.

The dear pre-Op nurse tried once, twice, three times and stopped. She said, *"Sweetie, I'm so sorry, but I'm not going to poke you again. I'll let them get you in the OR."* Moments later, a young, good looking doctor I had not ever met before strides up.

He introduced himself and quickly said, "I'm your anesthesiologist today and I'll take care of it no problem." I responded with *"Okay but I'm a 'tough stick.'"*

I kissed Chad one last time praying it would not really be the last time, and the new guy wheeled me down to the OR. By the time I got down to the operating room, I was literally shaking, there really are no words to share my fear of the IV, and I was dressed in a wimpy hospital gown...of course I was shaking.

But my sister-in-law, unbeknownst to her, came to my rescue. I remembered a verse that she had shared with me in a card and I started reciting it. *"My soul finds rest in God alone, my salvation comes from him. He alone is my rock and my salvation, He is my fortress and I will never be shaken."*

As I repeated those words over and over in my head a peace fell over me and I began to calm down. Good thing, because the anesthesiologist was about to prove just how little he knew.

"I'm going to put your IV in now," he claimed confidently and the warmth of the blanket they put over me was immediately stripped from my arm.

"Good luck," I said slightly sarcastically, but with hope too. Remember they had already tried unsuccessfully three times. He proceeds to try attempt #4, #5, #6, #7 and not once does it work or does he acknowledge me, although I can see the frustration on his face even through my misery. As he sticks me for the eighth time I began questioning whether or not he should be controlling my anesthesia. The eighth try doesn't work and visibly upset, he says, *"I'm going to put you to sleep with gas and a tiny needle through your foot and I'll fix it in surgery."*

"No," I virtually scream! *"Wait! Not until I see Dr. Reece."*

Now this new guy didn't know anything about me so he was on a steep learning curve and what he really didn't know was that I had a routine before surgery. After all of the process of the morning and before they put me under, I needed to see Dr. Reece, make sure he had had his Diet Mt. Dew to drink, (he wasn't a coffee drinker,) and I needed to find out what music we were going to listen to during surgery that day. Of course I would never hear the classic rock that Dr.

Reece seemed to prefer, but it gave me great comfort to know that he had been through his morning routine and with a Diet Mt. Dew he had a plan for the day, down to the very detail of the songs we would listen to during my three to six hour surgeries.

But as far as this hotshot new guy knew, I was about to say, "This new guy is an idiot, get him out of here!" Now after eight IV tries, I think that would have been perfectly justifiable, but I had no intention of doing that.

Dr. Reece walked in. I confirmed what we would listen to during surgery and that he had had his Diet Mountain Dew, then I turned to the new anesthesiologist and said, *"Now you can put me under."*

He inserted the last needle I would feel into my foot and moved it after I had counted back and fallen into a gentle sleep.

Surgery went well except for the typical pain regulation issues that tend to come after surgery as your body tries to cope and your brain tries to find its way out of the anesthesia fog of exhaustion and pain. I was still in foggy recovery mode the next day when I heard a knock at the door of my hospital room. Thinking it was Dr. Reece checking on me, I tried to sit up in bed and get my mind to focus. But it was the anesthesiologist who entered my room with a slightly less confident strut from what I had seen the day before. Even in recovery mode, where comprehension isn't crisp and weakness weighs on you like a heavy blanket, I remembered enough to know that I had never seen an anesthesiologist after surgery. He asked if he could come in…what was I going to do, run away? He sat on a chair in my room and said simply, *"Thank you."*

I'm sure I looked puzzled in my fully bandaged, half present state, and he went on, *"You taught me a valuable able lesson yesterday. You told me you were a "tough stick" and I didn't listen. I realized yesterday that with all of my knowledge, how valuable it is to listen to the patient. So I wanted to tell you thank you."*

I nodded, smiling, the picture now developing more clearly in my head, and remembering the eight painful jabs of the needle from the day before. The physical pain of those failed attempts has long left me, but what I will not forget is the way God gave me the peace to never be shaken and get through it, and more importantly, how He had clearly used that situation to teach the doctor a far more valuable lesson. I knew he would never again tune out a patient's request without giving it the attention it deserved...and for that, eight jabs were more than worth it.

PRAYING FOR BIG THINGS

During these years, I may as well have been a spy, I had so many different disguises. I had hats of every kind, but quickly found out that I'm not really a hat girl, with the exception of loving a baseball cap. When that wasn't my look, we decided to make it scarves. Not only could I color coordinate those with any outfit, but my mom could quickly make them from any fabric we could find.

My mother had graciously taken me to the fabric store early on to pick out favorite fabrics so that she could sew for me " fashionable" scarves fit for each occasion and every kind of weather. I had a virtual shop of my own when it came to scarves. They became a collection of sorts. My favorite was one a dear friend gave me. She had traveled all the way to Italy some time after my accident and sent back the most amazing blue silver scarf...it made me feel like I was walking a runway...and I loved it. So in the had transition years, as I had back to back surgeries to march my hair across my head, the shape of my head constantly changed, so scarves were the head covering of choice.

But then I found out my brother was going to get married.

Angie and Randy had met in college, both members of Campus Life and unbeknownst to me, Randy had his eye on her for some time. It wasn't until they took a mission trip together to Zambia, Africa (her for several weeks and him for 7 months), that their feelings for one another were solidified. Angie had studied architecture and interior design in college and was one of the most creative, entrepreneurial people I knew. She could see an idea in her head and help bring it to life with fervor and beauty like no other. I had only just begun to really get to know Angie, and she had rearranged plans to be at our wedding, knowing how important it was for Randy and us to have her there. But what she could see that both Randy and I needed was an encourager. My brother, having decided to study ministry, had been rocked by my accident and it proved a test to his faith. I remembered so clearly the Sunday before he left for Zambia, him telling me, *"If anything happens to me while I'm gone, be sure to tell mom and dad, this is where God called me to be and I won't ever regret going."*

As his little sister, that he would have already thought that through scared me, but we both knew what he meant. God was in control and Randy was confident in letting him lead. After my accident, that confidence was shaken. But Angie's wasn't. The encourager that she was, she would send cards sharing verses that stuck in my heart for years to come. And in one particular card I will never forget, she wrote, don't forget to pray for the "Big Things." She went on to say that we all knew God was taking care of the little things, but that we shouldn't be afraid to pray for the big ones too. It was knowledge our faith had given us for years. But claiming your faith and living by faith are two entirely different things. At this time in my life where I relied almost exclusively on my faith, family and friends to get me through each minute of each day, those reminders about God having the "Big Things" too were a welcome encouragement. Especially as I was re-growing hair.

Tissue expansion had been brutal. Eight surgeries to successively march what was left of my scalp across my head so that someday I would once again have hair. When we started, my head wrapped tightly in gauze, I looked like Sinead O' Conner. She had that beautiful musical voice I loved and was really the only woman I knew to have purposely shaved her head. But while Sinead looked beautiful and brave, my head looked scary and forced.

I mean let's face it. I was frightening. After tissue expansion started, the first time they held that mirror up to my head, there were no words. Just plain fear. It was bad enough I had seen the staples crisscrossed across my skull in the first months after I woke up. These foreign objects looked like small fruit growing under my scalp in odd shapes. The constant tugging at the skin meant that blood vessels would pop out, and sores would break leaving paths of scabs that were so out of place, the only comparison was the gross detailed costuming and makeup seen in horror movies.

At first I had been adamantly opposed to a wig. I thought it would look fake, and honestly, not knowing anything about wigs, I thought it would have to be made of human or horse hair. This alone freaked me out, but I also was NOT going to wear a scarf to my brother's wedding.

Although I quickly found a synthetic wig that looked as close to my old hair as possible, I hated it. I bought it solely to wear at my brother's wedding. Angie and Randy were engaged shortly after my accident and planned a beautiful outdoor wedding including my sister and me as bridesmaids. We were thrilled to be asked and even more excited when we saw the amazingly beautiful dresses Angie had picked out for the ceremony. They were a bright shade of purple and stunning to look at. Having dropped nearly 40 pounds, my frame was slender, almost too much so, and I was as I had become accustomed to, extremely paranoid about how I looked. The last thing I wanted to be was the one distraction to my brother's big day. I could just see people looking at their wedding album years later and saying, *"Who's the girl in the scarf?"* So I put that wig on.

I had tried on the wig several times before my brother's wedding to try to get used to it, but I never did. When the rehearsal dinner came, I was relieved to know that it was a windy day. Because they were to be married at a beautiful park outside, the rehearsal would require us to practice outside. It was far too windy for my wig, which even though it fit snugly to my head, still had a tendency to tilt the wrong way occasionally without warning. There was no way I was going to take the chance a chasing down a wig while we practiced for the wedding. I wore a scarf that night feeling much more confident.

The next day was beautiful and the wind had died down to a gentle breeze, so as I straightened the wig on my head with the beautiful purple bridesmaid dress on, I silently said a prayer that it would stay straight on my head through the wedding and pictures.

In a fairy tale like wedding, Angie rode up in a horse drawn carriage, having ridden horses all her life, to the aged and broken pillars of Pioneers Park. A new bride and groom glowing beneath the backdrop of the ceremony. It was simply lovely, and as the amazing lyrics of the song, "How Beautiful," were sung, two thoughts entered my head.

The first threatened the day. I loved the dress, and my wig looked re-markably similar to the hair I once had, but I was struck with anxiety over something much deeper. Staring in the mirror that day, I was fully aware, once again, that I was no longer the person I once was. In everything that matters I was. My mind was sharp, my smile was gen-uine, and my personality had not changed, but my confidence was crushed. My face was scarred and that was visible to all the world.

This song walked a tightrope for me. At any other time in my life, it was a beautiful reflection of faith, marriage and the love my brother reflected every time he mentioned Angie. But for me, it symbolized something much different, a definition I was forced to face on a much more significant level than before. What was beauty? Was it what I thought I believed to my core and what I had preached my entire life? Was it the heart, the smile, the gracious attitude? Or was there an undeniable outward element that could no longer be avoided as I tried to hide my scars behind this wig? Did people see me differently now? Did something else enter their minds? I had so many questions rushing around my head through one simple, beautiful song, and no answers.

The second thought that eventually won out was that today was a day of joy. And just as my wig was intended not to draw away from that joy, I was not going to let my sorrowful thoughts take me there either. I couldn't help but think about how beautiful it was to be alive, stand-ing beside my sister along with Chad, Nathan and my brother and new sister on their special day.

It had been literally years of balloons being implanted between my scalp and skull, then stitched together and then healing for weeks. Every week for the next two months doctors would inject saline in to them to blow them up. They would inflate to water balloon size, visible to the world as if you could walk up to me with a pen and literally burst my head into a million little pieces. Then it was back to the operating room for them to surgically remove the balloons and stretch my skin two inches further. My scalp would then be another mass of blood, scabs and stitches until it had healed enough to start all over again. Eight times I did this. Years and years of my life spent on trying to find a full head of hair again. I didn't even care what my hair looked like when I did have it, other than being clean and brushed. But now that it was taken away from me, I desperately wanted it back. It became a sign of "normalcy" for me...whatever that was.

I would wear that same wig at my sister's wedding soon enough, but as the tissue expansion surgeries neared and end, I longed for the day when I wouldn't rely on scarves and wigs to hide my head.

15
Through Blurry Eyes

Pain shoots through my head and I jerk awake. I struggle to see with one eye the display on my alarm clock...crap...wrong eye. It's been three years since my accident and I'm beginning to feel like there's an end in sight. Ironically, in the middle of tissue expansion surgeries, another complication develops. There is cataract in my right eye. My end in sight has grown blurry...overnight.

I didn't want to admit it was happening. The very common secondary injury for many burn patients was now my reality. I rolled my head so my left eye, my good eye could now see the fluorescent display that screamed at me 3:12 a.m. I read it as if it was a dare...dare to go back to sleep. Dare to think you could get a normal night's sleep. Dare to think the pain would subside enough to remind you what good dreams were all about.

When I was young, I loved a good dare. Not an out and out dare like when you're playing that stupid truth or dare game, but a real dare. A challenge to my abilities. If someone told me I couldn't do something, I was going to prove them wrong, In fourth grade when a boy said girls were slow, I outran every boy in my class for the mile run.

In sixth grade the gym teacher made it very clear that girls were not supposed to play football. So I played at recess. And just to prove he was wrong, I intercepted the ball to run it back for a touchdown. This astonished even my teacher as well as the boys on the playground.

So after my accident, when no one thought I would live, let alone walk, talk and think on my own again, I proved them all wrong. There is much to be said for determination and hard work.

But this digital blue alarm clock was different. It was a dare I could not conquer, yet.

I would wake up every night at 3:12 with a pain or symptom of some sort. Some nights it was blood oozing out on my pillow because my stitches had torn. At other times, shooting pain because my reconstructive balloons had too much pressure or a throbbing knee that had not yet healed. But the worst pain of all, it seemed, was not the physical pain. It was the questions.

On this night, it was two symptoms rolled into one long flood of tears. Pain, the unceasing, ever present, all-encompassing pain of yet another treatment to salvage what hair I might still have. And the more present long-term pain that lives secretly in my head.

"Why me?" What in the world did I do to deserve this? God why are you standing by and watching me fall deeper and deeper into this hole when I'm desperately trying to climb out? Where is that Hand you always promised to hold out to me? Where are your arms that are supposed to be carrying me? There are no answers in the dark hours of night. Only ceaseless questions and hurt remain.

I roll over to my side hoping to temper the pain of my head and catch a glimpse of Chad. I'm thankful that I've mastered the art of crying in silence. Hasn't he been through enough? Our life's plans are ruined. He didn't sign up for this.

Chad married a capable strong smart woman with her own career and a list of goals for the future. Now my biggest goals are to pull myself off the couch and decide how much pain medicine to take.

I'll call my mom in the morning. No wait. I'm not doing that. My sister? My brother? Hasn't my family been through enough? They fought so hard to stay strong for me, how can I show them how weak I really am now that I've come so far? My mom's given up everything... they all have. Their lives have been turned upside down because of me...I'm not doing that to them again.

I turn to God again. Okay God, you're it. You're all I've got so please hear me now! I'm breaking. I'm broken and only you can lift me out of this. So if you've figured out how to fix this, let me know, because you're all I've got.

I fumbled with my one good eye for the glass of water, choke down two more pills and pray that sleep will come again. While the night is dark, the sun always rises in the morning.

CATARACTS

The sun does rise the next day in bright amazing glory and I feel rested and ready to tackle the day. One more prayer answered. Boy that list is becoming long. *"Thank you God,"* I whisper.

My stomach lurches because in the mist of the tears I forgot to take something with my pain medicine last night and I need food now. I stumble out of bed and meet Chad fresh out of the bathroom ready for work. He kisses my cheek and saunters out the door promising, *"See ya tonight."* He may well have said, *"You're the love of my life and don't forget it."*

Chad is not an openly affectionate guy and sometimes short on words. But I need no words from him today, now that the sun is shining. For him this is done and we've moved on. *"Yeah, three years ago Kim had a terrible accident, but she's fine now and life is good again."* It's amazing and a little puzzling the optimism Chad radiates every day. He sees me the same way. There is no hesitation when he touches me, no second glance at my scarred face or torn up body and in the light of day I know it's true. To him I'm the same Kim he married and he's the same guy he always was. He is by definition, a hero to me, but to him he just did what anyone else would do. I know this is not true. So many men would've walked out the door at the first sign of trouble. Maybe wouldn't have even stuck around to send the end of the story, but not Chad. His optimism and can do attitude constantly amazes me…and sometimes puzzles me. It seems the vast differences I so often see in men and women are played out in our every day. Chad is always living in the present. Solving problems today. And I'm forever reflecting on the past and projecting into the future. I guess that way we've got life covered.

I take a few bites of breakfast, never a favorite meal, but I feel less nauseous and ready to take on the day. I sit down with some paper-work for a project I'm working on with the Junior League. There is a fulfillment that comes in focusing on others that is not possible if the focus is on you.

After Chad and I were living on our own again and returning to some sense of normalcy, although we were rescheduling our lives around surgery, on most days, Chad went to work and I kept a full schedule of household duties and at home rehab. I was just beginning the task of re-entering life, with the full knowledge that although things were different I could no longer define our lives based solely around my accident. I knew years of surgery were still to come, but spending my days with insurance agency calls, pills and sorrow was no longer acceptable.

It was time to make a decision about what I wanted to do, though at the time options were limited. I tried to go back to work, returning to the Lincoln TV station I had called home just before the accident, but days were spent producing and sharing with others how to tell a story rather than the job I wanted. Though I loved helping young reporters, I never liked sitting behind the scenes instead of in front of the camera. This also didn't take into consideration how difficult it was to be consistent there. Imagine telling your boss, "I have surgery tomorrow and will likely be out for at least two to three weeks recovering." Then imagine saying this about every other month. Not conducive to them or me.

It was just a year before that a mentor of mine had suggested I volunteer and give back.

I was lamenting the fact that I couldn't go back to work because of my exhausting surgical schedule, but that I needed to be out of the house and she suggested I join the Junior League. At first I thought that was a nice suggestion, but not really my kind of organization. I admit I thought it was high-class sorority all over again. I pictured white gloves, sterling silver tea sets and women who thought too highly of themselves. I couldn't have been more wrong.

The women I met were gracious, down to earth, generous, smart and amazing. All came from different walks of life. A vast array of careers were represented, and others were raising children at home. But as

I would soon find out, all of them seemed to have hearts of gold, wanting to know how we could help and have fun. It was the perfect distraction to be planning and working on worthwhile projects without the pressure of deadlines, knowing my deadlines were different right now. If tomorrow I was leaving for surgery in Des Moines and may need weeks off to recover, I could take them. There was no paycheck involved, only the best kind of reward.

No longer able to face my own reality, I threw myself into helping others. I have always had a heart for helping others. Working on youth group mission trips in inner cities and desolate towns brought me immense joy, Just bringing a smile to a sad child's face gave me back far more than I ever felt I gave. And my mentor's suggestion gave me the perfect outlet in the Junior League.

For years through the Junior League, I was able to join my friends in making an impact on others all the while distracting myself form the realities of my crushed career and devastating loss. It certainly helped to make some amazing friends along the way who encouraged me at every turn.

I've always known that joy that can come in helping others and as I lived out that joy after my accident, I knew that in part it was an escape to the pain of loss. I suppose there could have been much worse roads that I could have traveled to mask the sadness over my dreams and career, drugs, alcohol, depression, anger, but those didn't really seem to fit my personality.

I was just sitting down to my computer to try my hand at some publicity for an upcoming event, when the phone rang.

"Hello?" I said only to be answered by an unfamiliar voice.

"Mrs. Shrick? This is Anthony from the...insurance company with a few questions about your upcoming surgery." He said it so fast I had to think hard about who this was. Not to mention I had about three surgeries coming up and I had no idea which one he was referring to.

Oh. Great. There goes my sunny disposition. Yet another "representative" from the television station's insurance company. Great I'm sure this conversation ought to be good. Because my claim was a worker's compensation claim, this insurance company was all over my case. I had a personal escort to every one of my doctors' appointments. She would literally sit next to my mother, Chad or whomever was with me and listen to the doctors diagnose my next step. Then, often had the audacity to ask questions about the claim before I could even open my mouth.

I remember one day thinking to myself, *"Who is this women that's been following me around?"* I know my mom had explained who she was and I'm quite sure she must've introduced herself in the beginning, but I did not remember that conversation well. In all honesty though, I was too weak to fight that battle, so I obliged and let her intrude on my appointments. She followed me and my recovery for the months of my hospital stay and my outpatient therapy. And then one day she was gone. I'm quite sure her disappearance coincided with the time when the worker's compensation issue came up. The questions always was how long was it going take for a full and complete recovery in their minds? Thankfully that issue was settled and she no longer was my shadow.

But that meant the phone calls began. I lost my tag-a-long shadow and picked up a full time babysitter via phone, constantly calling to ensure that the paperwork I sent in to cover medical costs was accurate and necessary. It was truly a full time job making sure the insurance company paid their bills. And there was no point of trust. Every phone call was like an accusation of insurance fraud. *"Is this really necessary? Hasn't this already been taken care of?"* they would ask.

But today I was feeling generous. I guess it was this guy's job to call and ask me questions and I would be fine to answer the rote ones once again, so I responded.

"Hi Anthony, how are you today?"

"Fine Mrs.Shrick, thanks for asking."

"It's actually Mrs. Shirk. S-H-I-R-K." I spelled my name for him rolling my eyes and already beginning to be annoyed. You'd think after years of this on-going conversation, they could get my name right. They did have every medical record and intimate detail of my recovery sitting right in front of them in black and white.

"Oh of course Mrs. Shirk. Well, I wanted to discuss your upcoming surgery."

"That's fine. Which one are you referring to?"

"Do you have more than one?"

"Actually yes. I am having the second half of my tissue expansion surgery in a few weeks. I have a toe surgery that has been scheduled just prior to that, and I have developed a cataract in my eye so I will have to have cataract surgery and a lens placed in my eye."

"I see." He paused as if he were writing notes and I thought of the irony in his words. Actually, that meant I could NOT see. But I let that reference go untouched.

When he was ready to proceed he said, *"Actually it was the cataract surgery I was referring to. Can you tell me about it?"*

"Sure. I woke up one morning and couldn't see my alarm clock with my right eye."

"What exactly do you mean by you couldn't see?"

What? I screamed to myself? Did he really just ask me that question?

"Exactly what I said. I couldn't see out of my right eye. It's a very common side effect of burn patients."

"I see," he responded once more missing the irony of his words, *"Well what percentage would you guess you can see with that eye?"*

"I guess that would be zero percent. Everything is blurry and I cannot focus on anything."

"Well, what do you think your restrictions are exactly?"

"Restrictions?" I asked raising my tone? Was he stupid? *"I can't see out of my eye. Fifty percent of my sight is gone. This makes it difficult to read, restricts my depth perception of any-thing and it's hard to see street signs and drive."*

"Actually, Mrs. Shrick, they say that drivers with impaired vision are technically better drivers than those with full vision."

Are you &*%*&$^& kidding me? I don't cuss and I rarely raise my voice without reason, but I was about to launch the phone through the TV or window or anything that would shatter at this point. I was FURIOUS!!! And so for me, though it seemed perfectly justified, I had just hit a new low. The F-Bomb didn't even come out of my mouth but boy was I thinking it! I hadn't met Anthony, but for now he was enemy number one in my book. I had survived thirteen thousand volts, brain surgery, burns that left me scarred forever and likely had taken my career with them, over twenty surgeries since that day three years ago and all for what? So I could sit here on a perfectly good sunny day arguing with Anthony over whether or not I REALLY needed cataract surgery. A surgery for 75-year olds, not twenty-somethings. This man was implying that my cataract surgery was an optional surgery that it wasn't necessary and shouldn't be covered under my claim, and I had had enough. My head was throbbing, I wanted to hit something and yet I tried to compose myself.

What else could they take from me? Every ounce of privacy and dignity was gone, every ounce of energy was now spent recovering or justifying why I needed another surgery. As far as this insurance company was concerned, I made up this whole accident thing as a fraudulent attempt to become overly familiar with the inner workings of plastic surgery. This was bull&b?n$...there I went again...who was I becoming? Who was this person I saw reflected in the mirror every day? I certainly didn't recognize her anymore. Is it possible that I was becoming the monster I saw in the mirror?

"Well, Anthony, again my name is Mrs. Shirk, not Schrick. And in response to your insinuation that this surgery is optional, I'm

quite sure your facts and research are incorrect, but I would suggest you put a patch over your eye tonight and drive home to verify that you are indeed NOT a better driver when you can't see out of one of your eyes. My surgery is scheduled with Dr. Hassebrook next month. And you're welcome to call him with any further questions. HAVE A NICE DAY!!!" And I hung up.

As the tears rallied again, I made a decision. I would not let this kill me. I had survived the worst. I would survive this too. My body would be forever scarred, but my soul would not. This would be the biggest giant I could ever possibly encounter, the emotional battle of not wanting to accept what life had dealt me, but I would slay him with the fierceness of David.

16
Scarred But Beautiful

After years of pain and scarves and itchy hot wigs the day had come. My scalp was healed enough and hair had grown long enough to get some sort of haircut.

You would have thought I would have been excited, joyful even, but I was just sad.

Celine had cut my mother's hair for years and knew the whole story. I asked for a private room, more comforted at the familiar picture of me in a scarf than with my head exposed. It had been four years since my accident and I had become very adept at hiding my head. If I was not at home, and you weren't immediate family, you didn't see my head.

But today was the day to face my fears. I had become accustomed to the stares of strangers, scars on my face, surgeries in progress, but all the while I knew that my head would be covered, the hardest part for me was to see. So when I had to remove that beautiful blue silver scarf for the first time and reveal a lopsided uneven, scarred and still a bit scabbed head even to someone who knew the story, I felt more vulnerable than I ever have. I choked back tears wondering to myself why this picture that was supposed to be restoring me to my looks was not what I saw in the mirror.

We were supposed to turn in our proofs and choices of the wedding album the week my accident happened. Our Des Moines apartment was full of pictures of bliss. The happiest day of my life, you literally couldn't wipe the smile off of my face. And that's how I remember looking. I had watched endless tapes of my stories on TV, seen countless pictures from when I was a child for the last 25 years, and today those pictures dissolved before my eyes just as surely as if a fire was burning them one by one. This day, the day of my first haircut, I would face the fact that no matter how many years passed by, I would never again look the same.

Celine cut my hair that day. The mass of straggly dark brown hair no longer look anything like the long blond locks I lived with all of the first quarter century of my life. She did the best she could with a cheerful smile and kind conversation, but I don't remember a word of it. My mom stood beaming. This was a huge step and in my mind I knew that I should be beaming too. But all I knew was that I would never again look the same and the camera that had once been my friend, was now permanently my enemy.

17
Finding My Voice

In TV there are two kinds of television stories. Live shots in real time were exciting, adrenaline pumping and fun to do, but if I really wanted to make an impact, I wanted access to an edit bay. There I could take my time and write my story with care. Usually Live shots were limited to fifteen to thirty second spots interacting with the anchor desk, but taped stories could be anywhere from thirty seconds to two minutes, depending on the placement in the newscast.

I had trained for years as a journalist; analyzing the facts of a story and boiling them down to important details. The camera was my friend and the quick, objective, analysis of a situation came easily to me. Then again, I could fix anything in an edit bay. Cutting out excess footage, covering a bad angle with B-Roll (additional video footage meant to keep things interesting). But my story could no longer be edited to make it look better. There was no "fixing" to make it easier to digest.

It started rather organically as I received a few invitations to speak. A local church in Iowa asked if my colleague David and I would join them for their "Miracle Sunday." He would interview us and a few other people with stories of faith to share with their church.

Then my parent's home church, the place I called home for so many years and where Chad and I were married, asked us to come. They had been praying for us since the accident and so we joined them on a Sunday morning. I spoke at a Safety Stand down day at Union Pacific and an engineering firm where my good friend worked.

With each opportunity I had to speak, I was lifted up and able to see a new perspective on how my accident might be able to help others. Speaking was lifting my focus from what I had lost to what I had gained.

And it was with this attitude that I felt called to make sure that this never happened to anyone else in the industry again.

ATTORNEYS

I was still in the hospital one evening when I first saw reports of my accident on TV. By the time I had regained consciousness and had begun to understand what had happened to me, reports of the accident investigation were being reported.

Initially IOSHA (Iowa Occupational Safety & Health Commission) had fined the company I was working for several thousand dollars for safety violations.

I remember feeling vindicated, slightly, though I still didn't fully understand the consequences of their actions, or lack of action. I knew that my training had been slim and there were precautions that should have been taken to prevent my accident, but I didn't know to what extent. I saw these reports and felt good about the fact that someone was looking out for my interests. That was to be short-lived. It wasn't until weeks later that I learned the fines had been significantly reduced from severe violations to a mere slap on the wrist. The hardest thing for me to understand was that not one person had come to consult me about the infractions.

This was just the beginning of a long period of dealing with attorneys and the legal system. My father and husband initially consulted with some attorneys regarding workman's compensation issues and to research any other concerns apparent with my accident. It was a valuable step I could not have taken myself and I am forever thankful to them. While I was thankful to be alive, I was becoming angry. I knew that I had not been trained well enough to work with the logistics of a technical Live truck, and had even expressed my discomfort with that to the news director, who had left shortly after I was hired. And as far as advocates go, I could not have chosen two more valuable men, not only because they were the loves of my life, but because of how they were wired.

From the moment I met Chad, he was decisive and slightly impulsive. Never afraid to take a risk, and with instincts grounded in facts, his decisive nature usually paid off big dividends.

My favorite place in all of the world is on a beach at sunrise watching the tide roll in and the beauty of the sun as it peaks over the horizon. There is something so calming and reassuring in seeing waves roll in in such constant rhythm and in knowing that the sun always rises. This is Chad, always the optimist, always reliable and can always be counted on to find a solution, even if it's not always one I agree with.

There are trees on the plantations in Louisiana that live for 700 years. Their massive tree trunks are a child's dream. Some extend a full 30 feet at the base and as their full branches extend back to the ground, it's as if the tree is hugging itself. Living oaks is what they call them, never fully losing their leaves until the new buds have sprouted, perpetually green and welcoming.

My dad was like one of those trees...strong and imposing to any outsider, a protector of all that stood beneath it. And yet arms with the breadth to welcome anyone who came close with a strong embrace that didn't let go.

Trees like those aren't anywhere to be found in Nebraska but we loved our trees none the less. We would climb as high as we could gingerly stepping on those outer branches cautiously wondering if they could sustain our full weight. If they did, it would ultimately give us the gift of great height and new perspective.

My dad and Chad looked at the big picture and took a different perspective when I couldn't do that for myself. These two loves of my life, steadfastly protective of me, set me up for an opportunity to help ensure that this kind of tragedy would not strike again.

More than anything, I was determined to do whatever it took to ensure that this did not happen to anyone else. When I was able, I would come to find out that most people in my position didn't live to tell about it.

In February of 1998, I met my attorneys for the first time. They convinced me that first day that we had legal recourse for everything that had happened to me, and for me it was the first step. Filing suit was not an easy decision to come to. I spent many hours discussing this with Chad and praying about it alone at night. It could have devastating effects on my career, on my physical well-being and on my family. They had already lived through this tragedy once and I was going to ask them to live through it again. But I was sure that to help others, I needed to have my day in court.

We began the long process of research, interviews, depositions, and legal filings. I had never really understood why people were hesitant to comment on anything for the media, but I got my first taste. It was the first time I felt like the target of interviews. As soon as we filed I started getting questions like, "How much money do you want?"

Quite frankly, nothing could have been further from my mind. This was a lawsuit filed on principle and meant to prevent other accidents from happening, and yet every media outlet wanted to know about money. I was outraged! Two points with regard to money stood out in my mind in those early days of filing a lawsuit.

One, a couple of options could have prevented my accident. A safety alarm that could have been attached to the mast and even a simple insulation tool at a cost of about ten dollars at a local hardware store could have prevented my accident and yet these manufacturers who were designing parts for NASA hadn't made their LIVE trucks safer.

And two, there is not enough money in the entire world to put a dent in the damage, both physically and emotionally me and my family had been through.

The fact that this was so clearly a case of right and wrong in my eyes made any suggestion of companies merely writing a check and writing me off with their signature furious. And it only served to fuel the fire growing inside of me. So that question, "How much?" did three things. It infuriated me, made me incredibly attuned to making this case about more than the money for everyone and awakened me to what the next two years would hold.

I wanted to know everything. Looking back, I'm sure I was a pain to my attorneys because I used to read the legal briefs for fun...and perhaps rehab. I would routinely send back corrections. I would call my attorneys in Des Moines and say, "Hey Joe, on page three line 48 there is a typo." One time I even remember having them change wording because it said "Plaintiff Kimberly Arms prays..." Even after I was told that that was typical lawyer-speak, I made them change it, because I wasn't about to have people claiming that this is what I was praying.

Amidst all of this, there were doctors' appointments, surgeries and calls from insurance companies too numerous to count. There were emotionally draining and painful times of videotaping surgical progress, or taking pictures of hospital recovery. And yet through it all, I felt like I was doing something to help. I was calling attention to an unjust situation.

DEPOSITION

And then there was the deposition. Rule number one: Just be myself and tell the truth. Rule number two: I had been warned not to elaborate. If the other attorneys wanted to know they would ask. And rule number three: There was to be no casual conversation in the hallway with attorneys. Even if it was off the record, it could be submitted as "on the record" later. And so Chad and I kept our distance. There were 7 dark suits in the room that day, and me in bright red, in the hot seat.

As we all stood to take a break, I noticed one of the quieter attorneys hanging around as if he wanted to strike up a conversation. I'm a conversationalist and I love to meet and talk to new people, so it went against every grain of me to rudely and abruptly walk away from this man who really seemed to have something to say. But I remembered Joe's advice, and so we dispersed with few words and Chad and I retreated to another room. When the break was over Chad and I were headed for the conference room when the attorney appeared from nowhere again. And we were cornered.

> Without hesitation he began. "Kimberly," he said, "I remember the night of your accident. It happened not far from our house." He continued," I never knew I would be in this position of being opposing counsel, but I wanted you to know that that night, the night of your accident, the lights flickered at our house and we heard your story on the news. And I wanted you to know that that same night, my wife and I prayed for you. And it's great to see you looking so good!"

I believe that there live among us angels. On those days when we are unsure of where to turn or which way to go, He sends them to us. Throughout my accident there was an air of peace that God gave me in times of turmoil, and there were many. The anxiety of ongoing medical surgeries and then the physical pain I knew would follow. The physical exhaustion of facing another day fraught with unknown challenges and married to medications just to get me through the pain. The fears that haunted me mostly at night when my analytical mind and consistently led me to questions of "What if..." and "What will be...?" But at the heart of each time I asked for help, when I looked for light in the middle of darkness, He answered. Today, in what was for me the core of the battle I knew had to be fought, the day of my deposition, it was an angel sent to me disguised as my opposition.

I was speechless. This was perhaps the most nerve-wracking day I had faced, reliving my story with total strangers who were not necessarily out to help me, and yet this man who sat across from me gave me a gift I couldn't have imagined. I doubt he will ever know how much peace his words gave me that day. All because he had the courage to "corner" me and share his personal story.

18
A Mother Should
Never Have To

The trial was approaching and to their credit my attorneys were leaving no stone un-turned. They had compiled my medical records that now had to be wheeled in on a separate gurney when I went in for surgery, they were so big. They had blown up pictures of my entry into the hospital that fateful day, the scene of the accident and the tapes of my anchoring and reporting before my accident. They had sent news directors from across the Midwest my tape to review so that they could estimate "potential worth" had I not had this accident and been able to continue with my career.

This alone was a shocker. People who had never met me were laying witness to a twenty minute tape to dictate my "potential worth." I had always been taught it was impossible to measure. Everything was reduced to a dollar sign and the more "proof" we could provide that my life had in fact been ruined, the better off our case would be.

"In lieu of her employment as an on camera (reporter, weekend anchor, morning anchor, and/or evening anchor) Kimberly

Shirk's opportunities for employment in the news broadcast business would be restricted to off camera news assignments. By comparison to an on camera assignment, persons securing off camera positions may expect salaries which are considerably lower. Apart from this limitation, Kimberly Shirk has no training and/or experience in any of these prospective positions and it will/would be necessary for Kimberly to begin her career anew in 2002."

It was hard enough on a daily basis to look myself in the mirror and find hope, let alone when the people on your side were documenting every possible way to present that there was none. The worst day had to be when they wanted to tape the progress of my head surgeries. My mother, my favorite nurse, who had bandaged my endless summer skinned knees and wiped away my every tear when we moved from place to place, was now asked to do the impossible. To use her nursing knowledge and explain the facts about how my tissue expansion surgeries were allowing me potentially to re-grow hair.

I heard the pain in her voice as the video camera silently hummed in the background.

"Kim's head was burned down to the skull in the accident. They took a muscle, the Latissimus Dorsi from her back to then cover her head and reconnect the blood supply so that she might be able to one day grow hair again on the right side of her head."

I sat stoically as she moved around my head showing different angles of my mostly bald and scabbed head.

"They insert a tissue expander under the skin of the scalp and close up that incision. After it heals they begin eight to ten weeks of inflations.

During an inflation appointment they insert a needle into the port of the expander and inject as many cc's of saline as she can stand into the expander. Usually each balloon will hold up to 30 cc's (cubic centimeters) by the end of the eight weeks."

The strong dependence on straight Vicodin, no generic medications, please, jumped into my mind as she continued to describe the painful procedures. I would have to take two Vicodin about twenty minutes before my appointment. That way the medicine had kicked in by the time we reached the height of the injection pain and expanding skin. The pain was searing, but I vowed that each time I would push myself to the maximum of my pain tolerance. Ultimately, that meant the possibility of more coverage and fewer surgeries in the end. I understood by then that the more pain I withstood, the faster this endless process would go.

It's a strange connection, that of a mother and child, one I would not know for years. In some strange capacity, no matter how far the distance, a mother is always connected to her child. It's as if her heart was a marionette where her heart strings were literally tied to my heart...when the child hurts, that string is pulled so tightly and with such a jerking motion, you feel disjointed for a long time. Not only do you hurt beside them when they are hurting, but you hurt because you feel you could've done something to prevent the hurt or you cause the hurt to go away.

There was absolutely nothing my mom could've done that she was not already doing. From prayer to care, I could not have had a better partner. But the pain I heard in her voice that day (and later would see on the video tape), as she described what she knew was an excruciating process for me each time, was more painful to me than all of my surgeries combined. It may be that the heart strings of that marionette pull both ways.

19

A Long Road Through Iowa

Chad and I were in the car again, passing alongside fields of green, rolling hills and an occasional windmill, the winds of new energy beginning to sprout. We were again crossing the land of corn. We had traveled this road so many times before, if it hadn't clearly been a hazard, I was quite sure it I could do it blindfolded. Come to think of it, that jerk of an insurance agent did think I was a safer drive without eyesight.

For four long years I had traveled this road with one member of my family or another. Miles and miles of conversation regarding the everyday. We would listen to music until the signal failed and sit in silence contemplating the surgery to come, or the one that had just passed.

I returned to Iowa for every one of my surgeries those years after. They knew me, had my encyclopedia of medical records, and it's where I felt at home. Coming back for surgery now was like a reunion each time. I knew the receptionists who took the insurance information, the nurses who prepped me for surgery in pre-op, the anesthesiologists who would put me under, the operating room nurses, and of course my personal slew of doctors. When a new face appeared it was always a surprise to me, but considering I had been traveling this road for four years, it shouldn't have surprised me that a new employee occasionally came into the mix, but it did. It was like adding a new family member but not knowing about the wedding.

I was so accustomed to the routine at Iowa Methodist that when Dr. Reece, my plastic surgeon, primary doctor and the one who had seen me in the ER from the first day I came suggested I see another doctor, I was shocked. Dr. Reece had performed a full 24 of my surgeries in the last four years had suggested that I see another doctor, a specialist for my eye, and I was shocked. Dr. Reece could do no wrong in my eyes and yet he wanted me to see a specialist for my eye because I had so much damage.

Dr Reece had reconstructed my eyebrow and just about everything else on me, of course with a team of phenomenal specialists at his side, but he had in my eyes single handedly orchestrated my recovery and so I wasn't happy when he said he wanted me to see another specialist to reconstruct the shape of my eye. But I trusted him wholeheartedly and so even though the doctor he wanted me to see was in Iowa City, we went.

This was no easy trip logistically. We were living in Lincoln, Nebraska, now and the 2 1/2 hour trip to Des Moines was enough to try to fit into everyone's schedule let alone tacking another 3 hours onto the end of it...one way.

Chad was working for an amazing group of people at Norwest bank at the time and they had been incredibly gracious and flexible with my surgical schedule allowing him the time off to come for any and all major surgeries and this was no exception. So as the miles streamed behind us I was comforted knowing that Chad would be with me on this trip. I needed his guidance, his optimism and his ability to see something for what it was without emotionally being so attached that it clouded his initial impression.

That's what Chad was to me. My rock of practicality. When we met years before it had at first been solely as friends. He dated other people and I did too, always falling back on each other to be our back up date when I had a sorority function and no one I really wanted to take, or he had a night where he wanted to just hang out. I would hear all of his stories and tell him how crazy he was for falling for the latest girl and he would tell me I needed to get out more.

He was the fun impulsive one and I was the ever-practical serious one. We were opposites from the beginning, but we fit well. He knew when I needed to celebrate life and I knew when he needed a dose of reality.

This took some adjusting for my mom at the beginning of our relationship. In fact she was still adjusting to Chad and his sarcastic ways shortly after my accident. Chad was the eternal optimist and never let me forget that the sun was always shining.

BEACH COVER-UP

Shortly after my accident we were home and it was summer. I realized I would need to wear a garment of some sort to cover my leg any time I was out in the sun. No longer necessary to limit the scarring, my skin still burned too easily with such little exposure to the sun and besides that, it looked like shriveled cheese as the leftover grated skin hung from my leg instead of returning to its tight earlier glory.

I hated to go to the beach or pool. I had to wear more clothing at the beach than in winter, it seemed, and it always brought stares. People who see me now at our home pool are pretty used to it, but it never fails the first time I go on vacation or to a new pool to visit a friend. The inevitable stares, everyone politely trying not to ask what happened but expertly staring as if within my covered left leg lies the secret to the universe.

Never one to obsess over my looks, it now appeared that the stares of others forced a sort of permanent paranoia. It would have been, and still could be, a slippery slope of sadness if I let it be, but Chad was having none of it. Chad would do what I wished so many others wouldn't...he would point it out.

"Hey nine toes, let's go...the sun won't stay out forever!" he would say as soon as we walked into a new situation. This did two things for me that I'm not sure I've ever thanked him for.

One, it told me he didn't care about those things...he didn't think a thing of the endless scars crisscrossing my body...and he didn't. Not once in our married life has he called attention to the scars that race arose my body. In those times together you would have thought I was a swimsuit model, which I'm clearly not, just as every woman should feel with her husband. When I would be getting ready for a night out and be frustrated that my eye was sunken in and I had to draw in the rest of my reconstructed eyebrow, he would, as many typical males I know, just yell from downstairs, *"Are you ready yet?"*

This sense of normalcy coming from Chad, even though it wasn't reality for me, was comforting. And two, he literally yanked me out of the tunnel that would surely slide into the depths of irretrievable sorrow.

I've always hated the saying "a slippery slope," politicians using it to classify their latest and greatest mission, striking fear into the hearts of whomever bought into the scare tactics. It was overused, meant to induce fear and create a knee jerk reaction in the opposite direction. Kind of a like a tug-of-war gone bad after a hard fought battle. One full tug and the entire other team plummets to the ground often with mud or sand in their face, slow to recover.

But this slippery slope I understood. At times I was a step away from drifting into the "why me" zone. After four years of surgery, recovery and little time to feel normal again, I was tired. I had worked hard to recover and remain optimistic. At times I did it for me, and at times I did it for my family who had given up so much of themselves in every way. I knew this wasn't the life Chad or my parents had signed up for and I felt guilty about it, so I stayed positive and prayed a lot for peace, which was mercifully fully granted.

But there were days when the darkness crept in. Days when I could not fathom one more surgery, doctor's appointment, pitiful look or frustration with what was left of my hair. There were days when the mountain just seemed too high and I wanted to give up. Though I was nearing what would be one of my last surgeries, I was gazing up at Mount Everest. Frost bitten, exhausted with no food or water left and willing myself to take one more step.

This is how we arrived in Iowa City. Chad ready to check this surgery off the list of accomplishments and me seized with fear at facing a new surgeon. A stranger in a strange place, whom I was supposed to trust to cut into arguably my most valued possession, my eyes.

It didn't start well. We walked into the hospital and the lights flickered. You don't have to tell a girl who has survived a terrible electrical accident that that is not a good sign. I immediately asked Chad out loud, *"How in the world am I supposed to trust these people if they can't keep the lights on?"* Chad assured me they had generators *(What did you just say? I was supposed to trust generators while I was laid open on the operating table? Not happening)* and soon enough the electricity was back up and running, but that was no comfort to me.

I am a firm believer in signs from above; the sun shining though on a cloudy dark day; a stoplight turning red at just the right moment preventing you on being in the wrong place at the wrong time; a seemingly meaningless comment that resonates so loudly within your soul it sits with you for a week and moves you to pass it along.

Those signs lift my soul, give me pause and help me reflect on the meaning of life. But I also believe in bad signs and to me the electricity flickering and shutting off the very moment we walked in for my appointment was a sign that I should turn and run the other way. But I didn't.

YOU'LL NEVER BE NORMAL

I walked into that appointment with a deep breath and Chad at my side hoping for miracles. It didn't seem too much to ask. I had had four years of miracles and I expected the same from this doctor. I was about to be disappointed.

Every doctor outside of Iowa Methodist that had treated me since my accident had been thorough. They had to be. I had stacks and stacks of medical records; records of surgical procedures, infections, allergies, transfusions and every other intimate details of my life seemed to be spelled out in these humungous three ring binders. When they wheeled me into surgery with my records at the foot of my bed they would ask me to move my feet so they could fit the four huge binders on the gurney as they wheeled me out of pre-op. sometimes they just grabbed an additional gurney.

So if I walked into a new doctor's office, and I had a few times, they needed to study up on me. I had visited new doctors for foot surgery or cataract surgery, procedures I felt comfortable doing closer to home, but it required work on their part.

I was a textbook case on survival and I knew it from the early days when medical students would swarm my room to witness the removal of my trache. This relatively simple procedure was likely an unimpressive event for many patient recoveries, but I had not spoken for over a month and whatever words I might utter would make history in this hospital judging by the sheer number of witnesses.

But in Iowa City there was no review of records at all. Standard blood pressure, height, weight, *"What are we seeing you about today?"* questions were asked. I might have accepted these as fine, baseline investigative questions if I had not just been to hell and back. I'm not a prima donna and expect no special treatment on the basis of who I am for certain, but I did expect to feel like this doctor was about to take my case seriously and consider opportunities to help.

My accident had rendered my right eye virtually useless, and quite visibly so. I had not lost sight, fortunately, but had already had reconstructive surgery to rebuild my eyebrow from the hair on my head and cataract surgery to repair my eyesight from the very common side effect of electrical accidents.

My eye was pulled taught from the scarred, burned skin, remnants of the fire that had threatened my sight, but stopped just short. What I needed was a plastic surgeon who could preserve my eyesight, but re-sculpt my eye so that it remained open, and returned some sort of symmetry to my face, specifically my eyes.

After the nurses, standard, but offensive questions, I considered asking, did you even read my charts, but instead I politely regurgitated the past four years of medical procedures and explained that Dr. Reece had sent me here to see a specialist about my eye. She took a few notes and told me the doctor would be in to see me shortly.

I admittedly was pretty unimpressed, and in fact, pretty annoyed that we had traveled all this way and they appeared to have no knowledge of why I was there, but I could understand that they saw a multitude of patients each day and couldn't possibly keep track of every single one…especially the nurses, so I took a deep breath and prepared to meet the doctor.

When he entered the room, he barely glanced at me or the notes his own nurse had just taken and began with the same exact questions his nurse had just asked me. *"What are we seeing you about today?"*

Doubly annoyed with this same question and wondering why I needed to regurgitate my entire extensive medical history to his nurse if he wasn't going to even review her notes, I was already questioning the intelligence of this doctor. He asked me the exact same question and as I was retelling him the exact same story I had told the nurse, I was silently having a conversation with myself, noting that there were too many signs that this was not going to work, that I was not going to willingly let him operate on my eye.

And then I got punched. As solidly in the gut as anything I have ever experienced, but not with a fist, with words. The doctor looked me straight in the eye for the first time and said without hesitation, *"It doesn't matter what I do for you, you will never look normal again."*

You know in the movies when a character is under the influence of drugs or has been knocked out cold and is coming to how the camera will be fuzzy for a while and the sounds are muffled. Whatever he said to me after that point was silenced by the breaking of my heart. In one fell swoop, this doctor, this medical professional in title and experience had taken four years of miracles and hope away with one heartless sentence.

I had already decided he would not get his diploma-certified, allegedly skilled hands near me, but had no idea that he could take my last remaining breath. My world was spinning and yet somehow Chad guided me out of that office and back to our car for the return trip. As we made the long drive home, back through the cornfields of Iowa, my heart was suspended in grief.

We passed alongside those powerful windmills capable of exerting such energy and yet they were still, suspended from motion without even a slight breeze to feed their mighty power.

Today that's exactly how I felt. Empty, alone, with the wind knocked out of me...unsure of when the next wind might come and move me to overcome the devastating blow, to regain my hope, to find another surgeon and move to energized action again.

> *"See I have refined you, though not as silver; I have tested you in the furnace of affliction."*
>
> *Isaiah 48:10*

20
Settling For Heartbreak

VERDICT

I can still remember driving down 16th Street the day I got the call. After two years of research, legal paperwork, depositions, journaling, virtually documenting every aspect of my life, it was over.

We were set to go to court the following week, and while I was not necessarily looking forward to it, I was preparing myself to make a statement. I had been working hard with my attorneys to make sure every detail was accurate, to discuss what strategy we would take and map out the days in court: opening statements, testimonies from doctors and submitted tapes and pictures. But it was not to be.

A judge had ordered us into mediation to try to amicably settle this out of court and every offer I rejected out of hand. I vaguely remember my attorney and Chad encouraging an offer they thought seemed generous, and it may have been, but as I recall it included a no-fault clause that allowed the companies to claim they had no fault in the accident and continue with business as usual.

The rules of mediation dictate that in a good faith effort, each party has to either accept or reject an offer and then counter offer. We had been mandated by the court to go through this process and so, though I was frustrated with the rules, I was playing the game. From my vantage point, no one seemed to understand. Everyone once again was reverting to the almighty dollar and I could have cared less. I wanted industry changes, an apology and a chance to have my side of the story told. In a frustrated attempt to prove to them all once and for all that this was not about money, I proposed something that seemed outrageous, expecting full well to be in court on Monday. And they took the deal.

When Joe called me to tell me we had settled I almost drove off the road. I did pull over and cry, no sob. We had played by the rules and while so many would claim we won, to me, I had failed. My job was to educate and make changes in an industry I had now learned was fraught with inconsistencies. I needed to make it a better place for journalists to work, and I felt like a complete failure all because of the almighty dollar.

Now more than ever, in the midst of years of surgery to recover, I wondered what my purpose was. I was convinced I had survived to tell a story, to make a change, and now I was stuck with the same lingering questions. What now?

Two days later my grandmother died. Had I been in court, I would not have been at her funeral.

21
Silver Linings

MIRACLES

In 2002 I found myself once again in the familiar halls of a hospital. After 28 surgeries and four and a half years of planning for surgery, recovering from surgery or anticipating surgery, I was sick of hospitals. Everything about them disgusted me. The smell was sterile and cold. The rooms looked like prison to me. The procedures were rote and I knew them perhaps better than most of the surgical techs awaiting my arrival.

If I never saw another doctor in my life I would've been thrilled and you didn't even want to talk to me about Medical students. If one more person tried to empathize with what I was going through, observe me through the interested eyes of an eager first year resident, I might just jump off of the bed and deck them.

In fact, by this time I figured Chad had enough training to take care of pretty much anything I needed. He was extremely adept at all the mechanics of hospital beds. He knew before I even spoke to get me some water, or more likely, ice chips. He knew that my favorite part of the hospital was the blanket warmer, and there was no one faster at retrieving Jell-o, the only "liquid diet" solid I was often allowed to ingest.

Yep, I was pretty sure that Chad and I could get through anything at that point and I was pretty sure that in a dire emergency, he'd get the right people in the room before anything drastic happened.

Things had returned pretty much to whatever our new "normal" was. Chad was watching football, and I was in the hospital bed awaiting what was to come next. Pain would hit me on occasion and I'd reach for his hand telling myself, I had come this far, surely this would be a breeze. But what I was really thinking was, *"I don't want to be here. I never want to step foot in another hospital again."*

I closed my eyes and wished away the pain, letting music I had brought with me drown out the thoughts of the previous visits.

This had been an especially long visit, painful and it seemed to take forever before the doctor arrived. *"Lookin' good kiddo"..."hang in there"*...intermingled with a few words about the latest Husker game and it seemed like we would never leave. Then the dreaded med student arrived. Poor thing. She had no idea I was so tired of being observed, poked and prodded and that really I was quite sure I knew more than any medical student could possibly know by now. And so she thought she would help.

In her cheerful voice she started chanting through the pain.

> *"One, two, three, four...now breathe."*
> *"One, two, three, four, five, six... now breathe! Good Job!"*

If I hadn't been in so much pain, reflected slightly on Chad's face as I squeezed his hand, I might have hit her, but the doctor was ready, it was almost over and even as her counting seemed louder and louder, so was the racing of my heart. So much so that I couldn't speak.

And so Chad spoke for me. *"It's a boy!"*

With tears in my eyes, I took it all in. My husband cutting the umbilical cord, the doctor smiling, our son belting out a beautiful cry and being whisked away to make sure all was okay. And in a matter of moments, our first child, wrapped snugly in his blanket was handed to me. And miraculously, the pain was gone. Erased. Forgotten.

Our first of three miracles was born that day. April 9, 2002. In those tiny little fingers God told me it was going to be okay. And it was.

Epilogue

Nearly twenty years later many Silver Linings can be found...far too many to count. It's funny how life works out that way. Chad and I are still married, living in Lincoln, Nebraska, and raising three beautiful, intelligent, compassionate and wise-beyond-their-years children, if I do say so myself. Caleb, Logan and Addison are the daily reminders of light in our lives...bright lights we were unsure we would ever have based on my injuries. My brother, Randy, became a pastor and he and my sister-in-law Angie live in Nebraska as well, and have Cury and Praja (adopted from India) lighting up their lives. My sister, Valerie and brother-in-law, Nathan, an attorney in Colorado, are raising their three delightful daughters, Meredith and twins, Olivia and Milaina. We unfortunately lost my Dad to pancreatic cancer recently, but watched him fight a valiant battle to the end and know he is sitting, or more likely golfing, in Heaven waiting for the day we are all reunited. My Mom, is still the most courageous woman I know, full of love, grace, strength and kindness. She is my hero and always will be.

Our faith in God has only deepened with each passing year and I know I could not have walked the road with my Dad, if we had not been blessed with so many answered prayers along my path. No one knows what tomorrow brings. No one knows what trials await. But no one knows, either the opportunities unlocked by each and every roadblock, each and every obstacle. What I do know with certainty, is that light always wins over darkness. The sun, although possibly tucked behind clouds for a time, eventually peeks out from behind leaving a glorious *Silver Lining*.

Fire engulfed me in a matter of moments, and I was never the same. It inflicted extreme pain, and filled me with terror. There are still days when the terror returns. But it also revealed kindness I may have never known, brought me appreciation I may have never experienced and illuminated my soul with the peace that surpasses all human under-standing. So I choose light, I choose warmth, I choose to gaze at the possibilities when a tiny sliver of light penetrates and illuminates the darkness. And the scars I will forever carry will define a new opportu-nity to find a silver lining in the worst of circumstances. My children are my light. My husband is my light, my faith, family, and friends are my light. And may the scars visible to everyone on the outside be a badge of honor, courage, faith and fortitude for all the world to see. May they forever encourage each and every person I meet to seek the Light in this world, too often full of darkness.

Silver Linings List

Believe. Belief brings hope and hope brings life.

Surround yourself with those you love and those who love you back.

Dream big. Shoot for the moon. Work tirelessly. COMMIT.

Don't let the fear of "what ifs," control you. No one can read the future. Take a leap, work hard and prove doubters wrong.

When you change your outlook on your circumstances. A new perspective could be just a day away. Blessings abound.

There is value in being objective. Ground yourself in research, test the facts and not the emotion.

The eyes of a child give great vision and clarity. See through the eyes of a child.

Obstacles will find you wherever you are, but do what you love, despite the odds.

When the past looks stale, look for a fresh beginning. Turn your back on negativity. Choose optimism.

There is no red carpet someone is waiting to roll out for you. Go find it yourself.

Some days when you look in the mirror you will either laugh or cry. Choose to laugh.

Recognize when one door is slammed shut, another creaks open. It's up to you to put your full weight behind it and swing it wide.

Open your heart and eyes to new opportunity.

Find the sunshine. When it breaks through the clouds, you have your Silver Lining!

CPSIA information can be obtained
at www.ICGtesting.com
Printed in the USA
BVHW072118151222
654331BV00023B/1502